# CULTURE CATALYST

Your Competitive Edge For Unleashing
Unprecedented Company Growth &
Fostering High-Performing, Engaged Teams

**ISBN Paperback:** 979-8-218-58547-1
**Published by:**

Lead 360 Academy Press

**Printed in the United States of America**

**First Edition:** January 2025

"Culture Catalyst is a must-read! Its practical strategies not only improve communication, leadership, and emotional intelligence but also profoundly impact workplace culture. No matter your business size, this book is your guide to sustainable growth and lasting success."

~ Tina Saw, DDS Founder & CEO, Oral Genome

"Culture Catalyst isn't just a book; it's your personal blueprint to build momentum, enhance emotional intelligence, and ignite a thriving business culture. Packed with practical strategies and heartfelt insights, this is your guide to transform challenges into opportunities and your workplace into a powerhouse of positivity and growth."

~ Greg Essenmacher, Founder & CEO, GnA Consult

"Being a great leader and building a great team doesn't happen by accident. This book will show you how, step by step."

~ Katherine Eitel Belt, CSP, Founder/CEO LionSpeak

"Culture Catalyst book is a well-thought-out roadmap for building a desired business culture, offering a positive, research-backed plan of action. The authors come across as 'Healed Healers,' leading by example and inspiring others through their actions rather than just words. I believe this work will help readers uncover their 'Why,' transforming both their personal lives and the culture of their businesses."

~ Mark Thomasson, DDS, Founder & CEO, Thomasson Dental PLLC

"Culture Catalyst delivers invaluable insights and practical strategies to help leaders not only thrive personally but also cultivate a workplace where wellness and success go hand in hand. It's a must-read for anyone committed to creating a thriving, balanced, and productive organizational environment."

~ Eric Block, DMD Founder & CEO, Acton Dental Associates

"Culture Catalyst is the ultimate guide for leaders to build a thriving company culture and achieve lasting success. With actionable strategies to enhance wellness, emotional intelligence, communication, and leadership, this must-read shows that when employees are truly bought into the culture, extraordinary results follow—proving culture is the true key to business success."

~ Len Tau, DMD, Founder & CEO, Tau Dental Consulting, Head of Dental Vertical, Birdeye

"Culture Catalyst" is a great resource for leaders looking to drive business success through a healthy work environment. As a consultant specializing in software adoption, I've seen firsthand how emotional intelligence and effective communication create the cultural foundation necessary for seamless technology implementation and long-term success."

~ Jill Nesbitt, CEO Optimize Dental Consulting

"Culture Catalyst is easy to understand and highly interactive. My goals are to create a thriving, happy team, increase revenue, and boost client satisfaction, and this book has shown me that these aspirations are not only achievable but also sustainable."

~ Cassie Saquing Founder, CHS Consulting Group and Foundations Prep School

"If you're tired of merely surviving under the weight of stress and burnout, this book is the wake-up call and roadmap you've been waiting for—because thriving isn't just possible, it's necessary."

~ Kami Schatz, Holistic Business Growth Coach with a background in I/O Psychology. Founder & CEO, Efficiency Powerhouse Solutions

"Tiffany and Marni's successes through diversity are what make this book so valuable. The culture of your business is everything. It is what makes it work above all else. This interactive book will help you find/create your culture and this book should have a place not only on your bookshelf but on your desk to be a handy reference."

~ **Sandra Berger, Founder & CEO, CE Approved**

"Tiffany and Marni are your ultimate guides to creating a thriving success culture. Through their four pillars—wellness, emotional intelligence, communication, and leadership—they've transformed countless businesses by focusing on what truly matters in today's workplace. *Culture Catalyst* is an essential read for anyone ready to elevate their business and achieve lasting growth."

~ **Laura Brenner, D.D.S. Founder & CEO, Lolabees Career Coaching**

"Culture Catalyst serves as a powerful blueprint for transforming businesses into purpose-driven, thriving enterprises. It emphasizes achieving sustainable success while nurturing balance, emotional well-being, and a fulfilling workplace culture."

~ **Dr. Maggie Augustyn, BS, BS, DDS, FAAIP, FICOI,**
**Owner of Happy Tooth**

"Culture Catalyst is an insightful guide for leaders who want to build strong, loyal teams by creating a workplace where employees feel valued. This book offers practical tools to improve employee happiness, retention, and career fulfillment. It also highlights the importance of understanding generational differences, as what motivates one group may not resonate with another."

~ **Joy Lantz, RDH, PHDH, COM®, IBCLC,**
**Owner of Joy Lantz: Transforming Oral Health**

"Whether you're starting your career, leading a team, or redefining your company's culture, this book equips you with the tools to build a healthier, more productive work environment—and find balance in the process. If only this book existed when I was starting my career!"

~ **Zach Rosenberg, CEO, Zach Rosenberg Consulting**

This is a must read for those who want to elevate their business to the highest level by being a great leader. There are so many layers and parts that go into a successful business. Culture Catalyst is the book that will give you clarity and focus to elevate your business and life."

~ **Michael Yang, DDS, Owner, Tustin Family & Cosmetic Dentistry**

"To begin, how can you not love the title, "Culture Catalyst!? In this phenomenal book Tiffany and Marni will show you how to leave your current state of mind behind and create a new and super successful environment. They will show you how to create this! Fortune 500 here you come!"

~ *Robert M. Pick, DDS, MS, FACD, FICD,* **CEO, The Pick Group & CEO, Progressive Periodontics & Implants**

"I've known Marni for 17 years, and it's exciting to see her and Tiffany provide such in-depth guidance on culture. This book offers practical tools to make culture a strategic advantage and improve organizational effectiveness, benefiting all stakeholders. Having led transformations, I know the power of culture, and this book is a must-read for leaders."

~ **Jeff Tognola, SVP European Operations Cintana Education**

"In *Culture Catalyst*, the authors deliver practical strategies for building momentum in small businesses through team training and a focus on the core principles of a thriving workplace. It's a must-read for healthcare professionals seeking lasting success.

Wellness, Emotional Intelligence, Communication, and Leadership—*Culture Catalyst* breaks down these critical elements into a practical guide for small businesses. This book is a game-changer for healthcare entrepreneurs."

- **Bobbi A. Stanley, DDS, MAGD DICOI, FLVI, CDI**

# TABLE OF CONTENTS

# FOREWORD

## Nancy Smyth, LCSW

Founder & CEO, Holly Springs
Counseling Center

A core concept of *Culture Catalyst* is the importance of combining emotional wellness with business success. As a mental health professional, I believe that we have unique states of mind. We have a logical state of mind (practical thinking), an emotional state of mind (feelings) and a physical state of mind (physical health). If these states of mind are in balance, successful decisions and plans will occur. This holds true if there is balance in our personal lives as well as our professional lives. With the concepts outlined in this book, the path to a successful business experience is attainable.

*Culture Catalyst* does a great job at redefining terms. Challenges become opportunities. The ability to 're-write' your interpretation of a difficult or daunting situation can change the way you react. It can then change the outcome. Employees feel empowered when they view a failure as an opportunity. Leadership promoting this philosophy changes the whole dynamic of an organization in conflict. Giving colleagues permission to challenge their negative thoughts can affect outcomes in a positive way. Using the guidelines outlined improves self-esteem and can promote a sense of control and empowerment.

Changing from a fixed mindset to a growth mindset unleashes possibilities and gives employees a chance to explore their potential growth. In the current corporate environment, workers often live in a state of anxiety generated by minimal feelings of safety and no job security. The competition is furious, and workers often feel overwhelmed. By growing and encouraging a secure and safe environment, workers are able to become their best selves. The leadership places the emphasis on persistence and opportunity to achieve goals.

This book encourages employees to learn and grow without judgment. Leaders who actively support this approach encourage trust. Such an environment provides the space to learn and offers a feeling of safety and security.

*Culture Catalyst* gives solid tips on how to handle stress. As a therapist, I have worked with many clients who are embarrassed or in denial when it comes to stress. They work hard to hide it in the workplace, which often has negative results. The fact is there are successful ways to manage stress and they are carefully outlined. The fact is, we live in a stressful world, so I am grateful for the attention placed on acknowledging stress and then how to handle it!

Being present and mindful can change the way you look and see things. Marni places great emphasis on this simple but difficult way to be.

I wholeheartedly recommend *Culture Catalyst,* especially because of its emphasis on emotional and physical wellness. I absolutely agree with the authors' belief that a healthy balance of emotional and physical wellness has been missing components for success strategies. Creating an environment that encourages and expects workers to grow, learn and reach their potential is a guaranteed recipe for success!

# INTRODUCTION

Imagine walking into a room where the atmosphere is instantly uplifting, where everyone feels energized and connected. Feels great, right? You will experience this feeling when you walk into the most successful businesses. Whether it's a corner flower shop or a Fortune 500 multinational, a vibrant business culture is a key driver of personal and professional success.

Studies show that companies with strong cultures see a 4x increase in revenue growth and enjoy more team satisfaction. [1] Increased revenue and happier employees are the ultimate achievement for any organization.

We wrote this book for one reason: **to empower you**. We are here to help you transform your team, enrich customer interactions, and cultivate a productive, harmonious workplace. We bring four decades of experience working with businesses of all sizes. Together, we've crafted this practical, no-nonsense guide to help elevate your business to new heights.

We want to give you the tools and insights to elevate wellness, boost emotional intelligence, refine communication, and strengthen leadership within your business. Growing a strong, efficient, and resilient team will pay dividends for your business and give you a 360-degree viewpoint to take your organization to the next level. Using these tools could even enrich your personal life. We want to partner with you and your team to help change your professional lives with **the four key pillars** covered in this book.

Great leaders want to foster a pleasant workplace for their employees and an inviting atmosphere for their customers. When practiced and embraced, the four pillars can be the cornerstones that support and create this positive culture.

These four ingredients combined are a recipe for success. They can help you build a thriving, joyful, and positive culture with high productivity and low turnover. This type of culture means more consistency, improved customer/patient outcomes, and, ultimately, savings to your bottom line.

Entrepreneurs beware! This book is not for you if you believe your innate abilities are fixed and cannot be changed. If you avoid challenges, feel threatened by other people's success, or want to focus on "proving yourself," this book is not for you. We refer to these individuals as Fixed Mindset people.

If you view challenges as opportunities, embrace constructive feedback, get inspired by other people's success, are willing to step out of your comfort zone, and believe that talent is ever-improving, buckle up. Taking your already successful business to "best-in-class" will be an amazing journey.

We've got a ton of ground to cover, so let's jump right in. We want this book to be an accessible and conversational read filled with important concepts, stories, and resources. You'll also find many quotes from our favorite authors and thought leaders we have engaged with for years. We hope you find as much inspiration as we have from them.

# TIFFANY'S STORY

I've always observed people. Not just their actions but their emotions, their words, and—most importantly—what motivated them. My fascination with human connection and service has been the guiding force of my life.

Today, I've built a career centered on elevating culture in the business world. I believe that businesses thrive when their foundation is built on culture. It's not just a nice-to-have; it's the magic formula that drives success.

But this isn't something I stumbled upon overnight—it's been a lifetime in the making. I've worked in hospitality, dentistry, and leadership coaching, learning from both extraordinary leaders and those who missed the mark. My story is a deep well of lessons, experiences, and challenges that brought me to the realization that culture—and its four pillars of wellness, emotional intelligence, communication, and leadership—can transform lives and companies.

## A Family Rooted in Service

The foundation comes from my family. My parents lived and breathed hospitality and hard work. My father, an executive chef, worked tirelessly, always leading by example. My mother was a food and beverage manager, a master of event organizing, and the kindest teammate anyone could ask for. Together, they passed their values down to me. I wasn't just told to work hard—I witnessed it every day.

"Put your head down, lead by example, and don't get caught up in the gossip" is what my dad always said. My first lessons in communication and leadership began at home. Watching my mom graciously serve while holding the standards of excellence became a template I followed instinctively.

## Discovering My Gift in Hospitality

I started my professional life at 17 as a waitress. It was supposed to be a temporary move, a way to earn extra money while I figured things out. What I discovered was a calling. From the first table I served, I realized that authentic, heartfelt service was something I loved. Not for tips, though they helped—but for the joy and fulfillment I felt making someone's day just a little better.

Everywhere I worked, I sought out connection. I learned my regular customers' stories and made sure they felt recognized. People didn't just come in for the food—they came in for the experience. Soon enough, I was placed in the "premier" section of the restaurant, where regulars and high-tippers preferred to sit. The recognition motivated me, but all the while, I felt the strain of working under bad managers. The turning point came when I worked at an iconic breakfast and lunch spot, only to find myself in a toxic, hostile environment.

One morning, the owner screamed at me in front of the entire restaurant, chastising me for prioritizing the customer experience over a rushed delivery of food. When she threw a cast iron skillet at me, I knew I had to leave. That painful experience lit a flame inside of me—I realized how important culture and leadership were to any team's happiness and success.

## Mentorship at La Costa Resort and Spa

My life changed when I transitioned to La Costa Resort and Spa. This was not just a job—it was an education in exceptional service and leadership. Finally, I worked alongside good leaders who understood the importance of fostering a positive culture. At La Costa, I honed skills I didn't even know needed refining.

The thrill of working at a world-class resort wasn't just about catering to guests; it was about creating experiences that resonated on an emotional level. Celebrity guests, high-stakes events, or day-to-day operations—it didn't matter. My goal was always the same: anticipate needs and create an atmosphere of joy and relaxation. That attitude didn't just impact guests; it energized my coworkers. My actions rippled outward, setting a tone for the whole team.

I understood then that culture was less about policy and more about people. Passion and care infused into each interaction created results. It was at La Costa that I started to understand my ability to influence team dynamics positively.

## Learning the Ritz-Carlton Way

Eventually, I moved on to The Ritz-Carlton, a brand synonymous with excellence. On day one, I felt the energy shift. Every employee carried themselves with confidence, warmth, and competence. It wasn't just a vibe; it was the result of intentional onboarding, training, and ingraining core values into every team member.

The training I received during my time at The Ritz-Carlton is something I carry with me to this day.

I learned how to deliver exceptional customer experiences through the smallest details. This wasn't just about luxury—it was about emotional intelligence. Anticipating needs, listening keenly, and responding empathetically became muscle memory. That training didn't just help me excel in hospitality; it became the foundation for my philosophy on business culture.

## From Dentistry to Hygienepreneur

After returning to my hometown, my family dentist recognized my talent for customer service and communication. She offered me the opportunity to work in her front office, and I jumped at the chance. What began as an unexpected pivot turned into a lifelong career in dentistry.

Much like in hospitality, I realized that a thriving dental practice was built on relationships, trust, and culture. I applied what I'd learned at La Costa and The Ritz-Carlton to help transform practices as both a manager and a hygienist. I realized that patient satisfaction wasn't just about a great cleaning—it was about creating a memorable, anxiety-free experience that made them want to come back again and again.

Over time, I became a regional manager, running multiple practices and overseeing everything from staffing to creating systems that reduced stress and increased efficiency. My approach was people-first—taking care of my team so they could take the best care of patients. Those experiences planted the seed for my first book, *Hygienepreneur: The Dental Hygienist's Guide To Achieving Career Success & Personal Transformation*, where I laid out the blueprint for creating successful dental practices infused with culture and leadership.

## Four Pillars of Business Culture

Through the years, I developed a cultural framework centered on four pillars that I believe are essential for any successful business. These pillars—wellness, emotional intelligence, communication, and leadership—are the foundation of the strategies I now teach to businesses across industries.

- **Wellness** ensures that teams are equipped, physically and emotionally, to do great work.
- **Emotional intelligence** fosters empathy and understanding, which creates trust and reduces conflict.
- **Communication** is the glue that connects people, ensures alignment, and builds collaboration.
- **Leadership** sets the tone, inspires action, and models the behavior every team member strives to emulate.

These pillars aren't abstract—they're tangible, actionable, and proven strategies that I've tested and refined. Today, I help businesses integrate these principles to create cultures where people thrive and profits soar.

## Stepping Into My Life's Mission

My passion for culture didn't just appear one day—it was cultivated over years of successes and setbacks. My parents gave me the foundation, but my journey has been about building upon it and finding new ways to grow. I see myself as more than a consultant or a coach. I'm an integrator. I love rolling up my sleeves, getting into the weeds, and working alongside teams. I nurture, I empower, and I teach.

I show teams how to plant the seeds of a positive culture and grow a thriving garden where people are excited to show up every day. Whether I'm speaking at an industry event or working one-on-one with a team, my message is personal and real. I know how it feels to be in environments that drain you. I know the exhaustion and burnout that come when culture is an afterthought. And now I know how to create something better—something lasting.

## A Vision for the Future

Today, I have the honor of sharing my experiences with countless teams and businesses. Whether in hospitality, dentistry, or leadership coaching, I've experienced firsthand what an aligned culture can achieve. Businesses don't just survive—they thrive when people feel valued, inspired, and supported.

It's been a long road, but I wouldn't trade the years of learning, growing, and navigating challenges. Each experience has clarified my passion for helping businesses unlock their full potential through culture. My approach isn't just theoretical—it's lived, tested, and proven. Together, we can build foundations that not only drive profits but leave lasting legacies of care, excellence, and connection.

I'm here to inspire, integrate, and lead this movement. Together, we can transform workplaces, elevate lives, and create legacies of positive impact.

# MARNI'S STORY

I became fascinated with health, wellness, leadership, communications, and emotional intelligence in my early 20s, initially through an unexpected journey. It all began when my ex-husband's mother became an investor in a Network Marketing company called Nussentials. She urged me to join and was very excited about this opportunity.

I wasn't particularly interested, but when offered the sofa I had been secretly drooling over in exchange for signing up and starting my own network marketing business, I agreed and handed over my social security number. The sofa arrived, and so did boxes of nutritional supplements—every vitamin imaginable.

With my small New York City apartment overflowing, I took the supplements simply because they were there. I didn't know much about health or wellness at the time, but after taking the supplements, I started feeling better. I was shocked to figure out that those vitamins worked! This sparked something within me.

At the time, I was an executive working for a large advertising agency in NYC. I graduated from New York University and started my career at the age of eighteen, working in marketing and communications. After eight years in the industry, I began having doubts about my career choice. I was having trouble working for someone else and helping build someone else's dream. I also started to discover my spiritual side.

## Nussentials & Phil Mims

Gratefully, I had access to the incredibly successful leadership team at Nussentials, and under the watchful eye of Phil Mims and his team, I began to receive weekly coaching in leadership, sales, emotional intelligence, and communications. This was the seed that planted a deep desire within me to help others create financial and time freedom, and it created an incredibly deep-seated commitment to helping others to be healthy.

I began to crave more knowledge and began a quest that continues to this day. I began working with therapists, guides, and coaches, realizing that there was childhood trauma and other skeletons in my personal closet I had to uncover and heal if I was going to be a true leader and help others.

While developing my own skills in the four pillars, I began talking about how good I felt with friends and family and started. Within two years, I built and led a team of 2,500 sales reps down the East Coast. I became a national speaker for the company and helped countless others start their own businesses, too.

## A New Life in North Carolina

As I grew personally and professionally, I came to realize over the next two years that the marriage I was in was sadly not sustainable and I left the marriage to start a new life in North Carolina in October of 2009. I left everything behind to start a new life, which was one of the hardest things I had ever had to do. It took strength, grit and resilience.

My focus on the four pillars deepened as I worked to heal from a divorce and start a new life. Sadly, I lost my network marketing business during the divorce and sought to find my next business adventure. I joined Smith Advertising in Fayetteville, NC – a 25-year-old traditional ad agency that needed digital services. I began a digital services department for them and led the agency into its next wave of business success in travel, tourism, and healthcare. I was a highly sought-after speaker who discussed topics like social media, Google advertising, and branding.

When the agency unexpectedly closed, I stepped in to continue serving the clients with the beginning of my own agency, Front Row Communications, with a business partner. A few years later, I met my former spouse, Rick, who had a dream of creating his own holistic health and fitness center. He was a visionary, and I am an integrator, and together, we dreamed of building a place where people could experience 360 degrees of wellness.

## Dragonfly Health & CrossFit Center

I sold Front Row to my business partner and Rick, and we opened Dragonfly Health & CrossFit Center. We built this center over six years utilizing the 8,000 sq. ft to have 150+ classes per week. We had a yoga teacher training program, CrossFit, Zumba, a chiropractor, reiki, massage therapy, childcare and more. I received my certification as a yoga instructor, health coach and

CrossFit L1 coach. We had 1,000 members and 30 staff, and it's where I jokingly say I received my real-life "MBA."

I put everything I owned on the line to open the center, leveraging every credit card and asset I had to make this dream come true. I know intimately what it's like not to take a paycheck so I could pay my team. I remember earning about $25,000K that year, which was shocking, as I was a six-figure earner starting at the age of twenty-eight. I had to learn how to overcome fear, regulate my emotions and step into authentic leadership in a BIG way. I certainly made a ton of mistakes along the way; however, with each mistake, I learned and grew.

I wore all hats, including operations, marketing, and finance. It's where I also learned about the concept of hiring "fractional" people to help me, like my Fractional CFO, Ed Plackowski, with whom I credited much of my sanity in those early days. It was so hard at that time for me to manage cash flow and understand what to pay when based on the income we had coming in.

I sought to build a deeply connected culture at Dragonfly – inspired by the idea that in Italy, they actually have a Ministry of Culture that is entirely in charge of the protection of the Italian culture and performing arts, of the conservation of the artistic and cultural heritage and landscapes and related tourism policies.

The fitness industry is notorious for seeing high turnover of members with low retention and I worked extremely hard to sell each membership. I knew I needed to create an environment where people could find a home, build community and ultimately get healthier – mind, body and spirit. A "sticky" home where people wanted to stay and not cancel their membership!

At the two-year mark, I got pregnant with my daughter Sofia and learned through much trial and error how to navigate being a mom and a business owner. I also learned about the concept of managed growth as we grew very quickly and, after just one year, found ourselves outgrowing the space. People told me this was a "good" problem to have. I assure you, it was not. If you have people wanting to terminate their memberships because they can't utilize your services, you're canceling out all your hard work.

Six years later, unfortunately, the pressure and stress of being married business owners was too much, and Rick and I divorced and sold Dragonfly. It was the second hardest time in my adult life as I built that center from the ground up and it felt like my first baby.

More coaching and therapy and another fresh start into the world of Fractional Chief Marketing Officer led me into the world of working with health centers, gyms, optometrists, chiropractors and dentists. I was a coach and consultant creating custom solutions that created massive impact and drove new customers into these businesses. I began coaching and consulting on operations, culture, and marketing to help these businesses manage growth. In 2019, I had an epiphany and realized that if I wanted to help more people on a much larger scale, I would need to learn how to systematize my own company.

### EOS Follower

Thanks to one of my clients, Dr. Angela Tran, a weight loss doctor in Denver, CO, I was introduced to the book *Traction* by Gino Wickman and the Entrepreneurial Operating System (EOS). I became an EOS implementor for a few years before they became a franchise.

Thanks to Dr. Kristy Tart-Bryan and Dr. Adam Bryan, I had the opportunity to implement EOS with them and we learned how to modify EOS and make it our own for their optometry practice. We saw amazing results for them. Their teams' dynamics and culture got even better; they increased collections and had a happier and more fulfilling workplace.

**Fractional Integrator: Chief Marketing Officer & Chief Operating Officer**

Fast forward five years later and I work as a Fractional Integrator, Chief Marketing Officer and Chief Operating Officer (not just a coach or consultant), I love to roll up my sleeves and work alongside my visionary clients to help them get the traction they are looking for in their business.

I love speaking to groups about these four pillars we are introducing to you in this book. This book is the culmination of 25 years of "in the trenches" healing, coaching, consulting, building and development of both my own business and the businesses of hundreds of clients.

I am so excited to bring my life's work to you, dear reader. Thank you for investing your time in reading our book.

## *WE NEED A COMMITMENT FROM YOU!*

Our intention for this book is for it to serve as a living, breathing addition to your existing workflow. We didn't want to write a book you read once, place on a bookshelf, and never reference again. So, how are we doing this? With the "Integration Index." This valuable resource at the back of the book provides key concepts we hope you will integrate into your company.

After many years in the coaching and consulting space, we've learned that the best way to help businesses is not to quote platitudes and give orders. We achieve real results by rolling up our sleeves and working alongside our clients. So, while we can't physically be there to roll up our sleeves and join each of you, we're excited to provide you with the tools you need to start your journey with confidence. We want to thank Brené Brown for the inspiration in the creation of this integration index. We were introduced to this concept through her phenomenal book, *The Gifts of Imperfection*.

Now, let's talk about setting up the **integration index**. You can find the pages at the back of this book. The process is personal, and you should arrange it as you see fit. Feel free to write notes right here in the book. Make the integration index and this book your own. When you come across something important to you or want to remember it, mark it. Take time to slow down and consider how to apply the insights you glean to your business operation.

**Here are some categories to get you started:**

- Short-term ideas to implement (30 days or less)
- Long-term ideas to implement (90 days or more)
- Things I want to research more
- Quotes I'd like to remember
- Takeaways

Let's face it: very few businesses are solo acts. This book will be even more transformative when you share it with your team. We encourage you to read through it together, like a book club, then discuss it and brainstorm. We also offer training courses you can use with the content to help you hit the ground running. Let us be clear: we are integrators through and through, which means we don't want to just "tell" you what to do and then leave you to execute it all on your own. We want you to truly integrate this work into your business.

We've spent a ton of time working, testing and validating our "What's Your Workplace Vibe" quiz to help you align and get a baseline of where your company culture currently stands before going any further in this book. This free online instrument will allow you to assess your strengths and opportunities for growth around the main topics of this book before you start reading. It's useful to engage with it after you read the book. However, we feel it's more helpful to have a baseline of knowing where your skill currently is and where you need help.

Visit https://culturecatalystbook.com/quizzes/ to take your FREE "What's Your Workplace Vibe."

We have other integration tools for you as well, such as keynote speaking, workshops, and events.

Our 1-year course for teams called Lead360 Academy is available to help do the work for you. It delivers two 5-minute training videos weekly for one year to your team through our App or website. It's FUN as there is gamification to keep your team engaged, reporting to keep your teams accountable, and clinical teams can receive CE for it as well. You can learn more at CultureCatalystBook.com. Let's dig deep together to create real and lasting change.

**Challenging Company Cultures: So how did we get here?**

Company culture is the "heartbeat" of an organization—**the collective values, beliefs, behaviors, and practices** that define how employees interact with each other and with the outside world. However, despite its critical importance in driving organizational success, fostering a healthy and effective company culture remains one of the most challenging tasks for businesses. But *why?*

Understanding why company culture is such a complex and challenging aspect of modern business is essential for leaders and managers aiming to cultivate an environment that drives innovation, engagement, and long-term success.

While the financial performance of a company can be assessed with metrics, culture is much harder to quantify. For example, how do you measure "trust" between teams or the alignment between personal and organizational values? Because of its intangible nature, culture can be difficult to define, assess, and track over time.

This lack of a clear, measurable framework makes it challenging for companies to know if their culture is progressing in the right direction or if it's fostering the outcomes they desire. It can feel elusive—like trying to catch a cloud—and this uncertainty often leads to frustration, confusion, and misalignment in organizational efforts.

Company culture also needs to align with business strategy and goals. When culture and strategy don't align, it can create tension, confusion, and even resentment among employees who are unsure of the company's direction or values.

**But, again...*why* specifically is creating a great culture so difficult to achieve?**

- Company culture is notoriously resistant to change. Changing culture involves altering deeply ingrained behaviors, attitudes, and beliefs that have developed over time.
- When leaders attempt to introduce new cultural norms or values, they can face significant pushback.
- Leaders may fail to model the desired cultural attributes, creating a disconnect between what leaders say and what they do.

- Leadership turnover can destabilize company culture.
- Multiple generations and cultural backgrounds coexist in the same workplace.
- The rise of remote work, coupled with globalization.
- Attracting and retaining the right talent can be challenging and is intrinsically linked to creating a positive culture.

Company culture is a complex and multi-dimensional aspect of business that can shape everything from employee engagement to organizational performance. The challenges of defining, building, and maintaining a strong and effective culture are significant, but they are not insurmountable.

Ultimately, while shaping company culture is undoubtedly challenging, it is also one of the most powerful tools for creating a workplace where employees **thrive, collaborate, and contribute** to the overall success of the business.

And, you are in good hands. Yes, it's all very difficult. Yes, it takes time. But there are tried and true methods for making the changes you need to embark upon. We are going to help you get there.

CULTURE CATALYST is *your bible* on how to start creating a world-class company culture **today**…So, let's get into it!

# SECTION I
## WELLNESS

# EMBRACING WELLNESS

## Introduction to Wellness in the Workplace

*"Our environment is a non-stop triggering mechanism whose impact on our behavior is too significant to be ignored."* – **Marshall Goldsmith**

*"Wellness is the optimal state of health of individuals and groups. There are two focal concerns: the realization of the fullest potential of an individual physically, psychologically, socially, spiritually, and economically, and the fulfillment of one's role expectations in the family, community, place of worship, workplace, and other settings."* [2] University of Chicago

## Health

- Health focuses on the physical ailments one may or may not be experiencing.
- Wellness goes beyond health - absence of disease is one of the requirements for wellness.**

## Wellbeing

- Wellbeing is often referred to as "the balance-point between an individual's resources and the challenges he or she faces."**

## Quality of Life

- Quality of life pertains to one's perception of their health and life as a whole.
- The World Health Organization offers its own assessment for this: WHOQOL

Consider what work was like in the 1950s. Offices were extremely formal and hierarchical. From a wellness perspective, smoking and drinking in your office were quite acceptable and common. Imagine that! During that time, women and minorities died at unprecedented rates from lung cancer and other smoking-related diseases. Amy Vanderbilt's 1958 Complete Book of Etiquette even described workplace smoking etiquette. This time was also marked by workers harmed by accidents and asbestos. Anyone who has seen the hit television show *Mad Men* knows that the three-Martini lunch was a normal part of the workday. Blessedly, in 1964, the US Surgeon

General issued a report directly linking cigarette smoking to serious health conditions, which was the first blow to cigarette smoking.

There is more good news. We can trace many workplace fitness programs we enjoy today to executive fitness programs that started after World War II. On-site gyms and other benefits were primarily available only to senior-level executives, which increased the awareness of employee wellness. The 1950s saw the advent of formal corporate wellness programs, such as employee assistance programs (EAPs). Companies began to offer wellness interventions primarily focused on alcoholism and mental health issues through these programs.[3]

In 1970, Congress passed the Occupational Safety and Health Act, which created the Occupational Safety and Health Administration (OSHA) and called attention to worker well-being. This act began to shift responsibility for the cost of healthcare from individuals and the government to employers. As companies discovered the link between an employee's unhealthy habits and the increased cost of healthcare, they realized that improving employee wellness could improve the bottom line.

The Employee Retirement Income Security Act (ERISA), signed into law in 1974, went further, establishing minimum standards for private industry health care and pension plans.

In 1979, Johnson & Johnson established the first on-site wellness program, "Live for Life." This program educated employees on stress management, nutrition, and weight control and provided support for high-risk behavior such as alcohol or substance abuse.

In the 1980s, support for many corporate health initiatives also shifted. Companies began to focus on psychological well-being as part of their workplace wellness initiatives. In 1986, OSHA codified this change and began to encourage the implementation of mental health programs in the workplace. It aimed to address the issue of work-related mental health disorders (mainly focused on stress-related illness). Thus, work-life balance was born in the 1980s, and corporate wellness programs became a regular part of the workplace.

We can also thank Jane Fonda for making these initiatives popular and mainstream. Fonda's message was aspirational and approachable: Anyone could change their body and life. Her outfit, leotard, leggings, and leg warmers became the workout uniform de rigueur for 1980s wellness. Don't worry. We're not suggesting you and your team revive the leotard, leggings, and leg warmer era. Instead, we're all about keeping things inspiring, educational, and accessible for everyone.

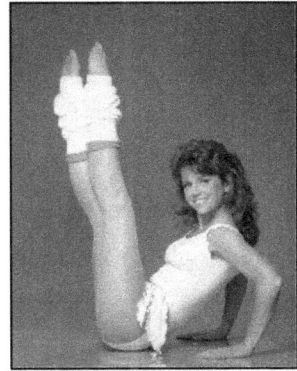

In 1990, the federal government launched *Healthy People 2000. This* initiative proposed that 75% of employers with 50 or more workers should offer health promotion services as a benefit. Though it was based mostly on anecdotal evidence, many managers accepted that workplace health promotion benefits a company by positively impacting employees.[4] In 1991, the National Institute of Mental Health launched another initiative, Managing Depression in the Workplace. [5]

Workplace initiatives during this period primarily focused on awareness. Companies provided classes, posters, and health fairs to encourage employees to make lifestyle changes, such as stopping smoking. Referencing a 2008 employer health benefits survey, 70% of large U.S. companies had workplace wellness programs. Companies like Skype, Google, Facebook, Twitter, and YouTube were launching or expanding their operations, a sign of dramatic technological changes worldwide.[6]

The wellness journey continued into the second decade of the 21st century, moving into a preventative perspective for various health conditions. Many employee wellness programs include health risk assessments and screenings for various chronic conditions.

In 2020, employee wellness was put to the ultimate test as we faced a global pandemic. Aside from the tremendous health risks, the pandemic left suffering, isolation, instability, stress, and distress in its wake. This only magnified the need for mental and behavioral health services. Today, we increasingly understand that wellness in all aspects must be a priority for every business, small or large.

Over the last few decades, large corporations have provided more workplace wellness options and used monetary rewards to incentivize employees to stay well. However, small businesses need to catch up. Smaller budgets, different business strategies, and employee considerations make it challenging for smaller firms to offer these programs. According to one study, only 7% of small businesses offer employee wellness programs.[7]

Health promotion must be related to overall company success-related factors, usually financial success. [8] Workplace wellness programs significantly improve many factors, including employee productivity, recruitment, and retention. These benefits outweigh the quantifiable healthcare costs.

HISTORY OF WORKPLACE WELLNESS TIMELINE — MICHAELRUCKER.COM

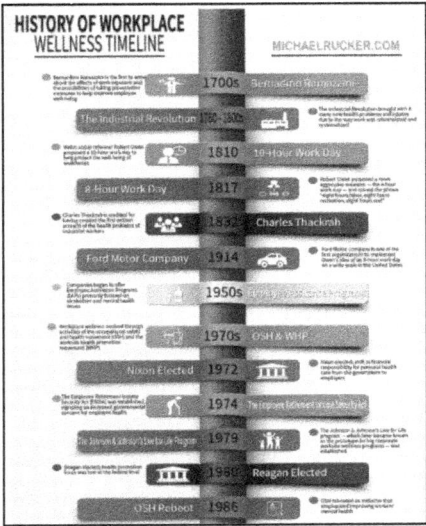

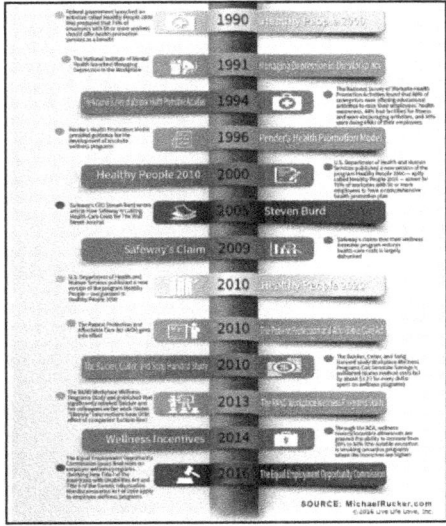

Senior management and human resources professionals are typically the final decision-makers on wellness programs and need relevant health promotion information. We sincerely hope that every small business owner and employee who reads this book will consider making wellness an integral part of their organization's daily workflow.

Let's discuss how you integrate and make wellness a part of your everyday workflow. We know and understand how difficult it is to fit in "another thing" in your already busy workday. So the question is how?

**Getting Started**

As goes the leadership team goes the rest of your organization. When you are ready to make wellness a part of your everyday workflow, you need to begin by helping your team understand the why and then how you are going to make this actionable. So many people talk a good game and have great intentions but then fall flat when it comes to actually delivering on the promise.

Begin by getting curious and during a team meeting or huddle, bring up the idea that you'd like to start incorporating more wellness initiatives into your organization.

## Setting Goals

Talk with your team and ask them where you would all like to be collectively as a team and then what their personal goals are with wellness in the next year. Set three to five BIG goals. Then, discuss which of those goals everyone will tackle each quarter. We love living in a 90-day world. Decide who will be accountable and how you will keep track of the accountability.

Will you do weekly check-ins? Bi-weekly check-ins? Remember, there is a difference between accountability and responsibility. The person who is accountable is ultimately responsible for getting the goal accomplished; however, they can delegate sub-tasks to other team members to be responsible for.

For example, let's say you decide a companywide initiative is to become more ergonomic with workstations. The next action item is in what quarter will you tackle this? Who is ultimately accountable for making it happen, and by what date do these things need to happen?

What subtasks need to be delegated to achieve this, such as:

☐ **Assess Needs**

- Conduct employee surveys to identify pain points.
- Perform workstation evaluations to assess current setups.

☐ **Research & Planning**

- Identify ergonomic equipment options (e.g., chairs, desks, monitor stands).
- Create a budget for equipment and implementation.

☐ **Stakeholder Alignment**

- Present findings and proposals to leadership for approval.
- Coordinate with IT and facilities teams for setup logistics.

☐ **Implementation**

- Procure ergonomic equipment.
- Schedule and oversee equipment installation or upgrades.

☐ **Training & Education**

- Develop resources or training on proper ergonomic practices.
- Host workshops or provide one-on-one coaching as needed.

☐ **Monitor & Evaluate**

- Collect feedback on new setups to ensure satisfaction and effectiveness.
- Make adjustments or improvements based on feedback.

The intention is not for anybody to be perfect but for every individual to progress along their unique road map to wellness. For leadership, it's essential to incorporate progress into a business's day-to-day workflow.

# The Wellness Blueprint

The "Wellness Blueprint" is your ultimate roadmap to total wellness. Each of us is on a unique journey; progress isn't a competition. In the next section, you'll find a link to a "pre-quiz," which will help you create your own Wellness Blueprint.

Look, each of us travels through various stages and experiences. Comparing ourselves to others can hinder growth. We are all unique. Cultivating a growth mindset is essential for personal development.

A fixed mindset is the belief that abilities, intelligence, and talents are innate and unchangeable, leading individuals to avoid challenges, fear failure, and give up easily when faced with obstacles.

In contrast, a growth mindset is the belief that abilities can be developed through effort, learning, and persistence, encouraging individuals to embrace challenges, view failure as an opportunity to grow, and continually strive for improvement. This distinction influences how people approach goals, setbacks, and personal development.

We encourage you to adopt a growth mindset as you endeavor into your wellness journey. Think about how you can weave the eight dimensions of wellness into your everyday life. Embrace the process, take it one step at a time, and let your path to wellness evolve naturally.

**PROTIP**: Focus on progress, not perfection. Everybody has different priorities and needs that create demand in their lives. Your wellness plan needs to be unique to your own set of circumstances.

# The Eight Dimensions of Wellness

- Physical Wellness
- Emotional Wellness
- Occupational Wellness
- Social Wellness
- Spiritual Wellness
- Intellectual Wellness
- Environmental Wellness
- Financial Wellness

Before we discuss the dimensions in detail, we invite you to take this free quiz to evaluate your Wellness baseline and help you focus on your growth areas:

https://culturecatalystbook.com/quizzes/personal-wellness-assessment/

\* \* \*

Physical wellness in the workplace is a key component of the eight dimensions of wellness. Employers that emphasize maintaining a healthy body and promoting overall physical health end up with healthier, happier employees who are more productive.

# Key Aspects of Physical Wellness in the Workplace:

1. **Exercise and Activity:** Encouraging regular physical activity by providing fitness classes, walking meetings, or access to gym facilities helps employees stay active and manage stress.

2. **Ergonomics:** Ensuring that workspaces promote good posture and reduce strain on the body is essential. Employers should provide adjustable desks, ergonomic chairs, and proper computer setups.

3. **Nutrition:** Promoting healthy eating habits by offering nutritious snacks, healthy meal options, and nutrition education can enhance employees' energy levels and overall health.

4. **Health Screenings:** Providing access to regular health screenings and wellness programs helps employees monitor their health, identify risks, and take preventive measures.

5. **Mental and Emotional Support:** Workplaces should also provide resources for stress management, mental health support, and work-life balance.

6. **Safe Environment:** Ensuring a safe and clean workplace reduces the risk of injury and illness, contributing to the overall physical well-being of employees.

By fostering physical wellness in the workplace, organizations can enhance employee morale, increase productivity, reduce absenteeism, and create a healthier work environment, ultimately contributing to the overall well-being of their workforce.

## Maslow's Hierarchy of Needs

Abraham Maslow was an American psychologist who developed a hierarchy of needs to explain human motivation. According to Maslow, human needs were arranged in a hierarchy, with physiological (survival) needs at the bottom and the more creative and intellectually oriented 'self-actualization' needs at the top. His theory suggested that people must meet their basic needs before they move up the hierarchy to pursue higher needs.[9]

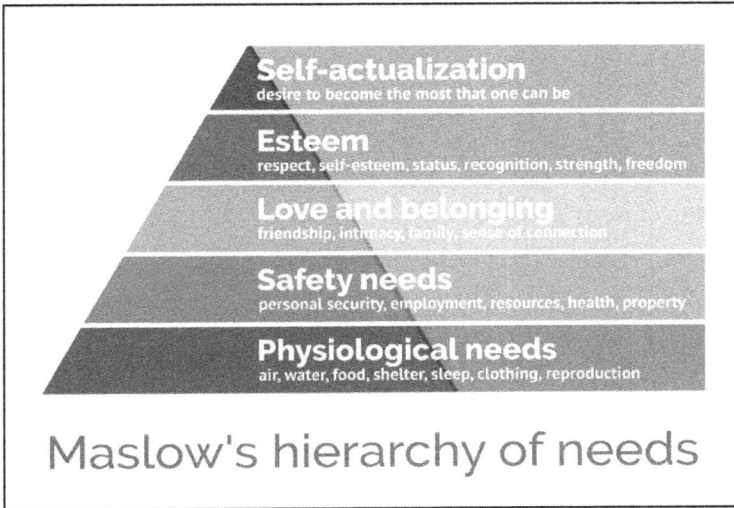

Maslow's hierarchy of needs

1. **Survival:** Physical survival is the core of our existence. For instance, we must have food and water or perish. Therefore, we will risk our safety to get them.

2. **Security and Safety:** After an individual's physiological needs are satisfied, the focus shifts to the need for security and safety. These needs encompass emotional security, financial stability (such as employment and social welfare), law and order, freedom from fear, social stability, property, health, and protection from accidents and injuries. Family and society often meet safety needs, including institutions like the police, schools, businesses, and healthcare.

3. **Love and Belonging:** Once physiological and safety needs are satisfied, the next level involves social needs, which center around feelings of belonging. Examples include friendship, intimacy, trust, acceptance, and the giving and receiving of affection and love. This need is especially pronounced in childhood and can sometimes take precedence over safety, as seen in children who cling to abusive parents.

4. **Esteem Needs:** The desire for acceptance often drives people to pursue careers or hobbies that provide recognition, contributing to their sense of value. Low self-esteem or feelings of inferiority may arise from imbalances at this level. Maslow noted that the need for respect is particularly important for children and adolescents and often precedes genuine self-esteem.

5. **Self-Actualization Needs:** This need is about achieving what one can become. Maslow describes it as the desire to accomplish everything and fulfill one's potential. Although Maslow believed that true self-actualization is rare, he acknowledged that everyone experiences fleeting moments, often called 'peak experiences,' associated with significant life events like childbirth, sporting successes, or academic achievements.

What does this mean for us? Team members need to be able to check off each of the items in the hierarchy of needs before they can start to focus on their physical health. Ensuring you have created an environment where people have psychological safety, feel love and belonging, support good self-esteem, and some form of self-actualization sets the baseline.

One's mindset is often the biggest obstacle to getting started. Dedicating ten to twenty minutes daily to walking or stretching can lead to meaningful change. This practice is beneficial for physical health and significantly reshapes neural pathways in the brain.

Neuroscience research emphasizes the importance of mental shifts in retraining the brain. Consistent practices, such as positive affirmations and mirror work, can have profound effects. In her book *You Can Heal Your Life,* Louise Hay, a pioneering figure in self-help, recommends standing in front of a mirror and repeating affirming positive thoughts aloud.

**How to do this?**

Stand in front of a mirror, looking deeply into your own eyes, and speak positive affirmations. This practice helps you cultivate self-love, heal negative beliefs, and build a deeper connection with yourself. By repeating affirmations such as "I am worthy" or "I love and accept myself exactly as I am," mirror work allows you to confront self-doubt, release limiting thoughts, and foster inner healing.

Starting with just a few minutes a day, this simple yet transformative technique can help reframe your mindset and empower personal growth. This practice can also enhance self-love and acceptance. This technique, combined with an understanding of neuroscience, shows that one can consistently achieve transformative results in overall wellness.

# Visualization is Powerful

Even after losing a significant amount of weight, it took nearly three years for Tiffany to accept her new physical state. In her mind, she still saw herself as overweight and inadequate. Despite others telling her she looked healthy, Tiffany struggled to see herself that way. She consciously decided to reshape her self-image by affirming who she was now. Standing in front of the mirror, she would repeat affirmations like, "You are fit, you are healthy, you have overcome," multiple times a day. This helped her recognize the person she had become rather than clinging to the past.

Tiffany understood the power of the mind—it could either lead her down the wrong path or toward growth and positivity. For her, standing in front of the mirror was essential. It was as if she was instructing her mind, much like a computer, to reset and acknowledge the reality of who she was meant to be.

# Physical Wellness at Work

The average person spends more time working than any other daily activity. Over a lifetime, this can add up to 90,000 hours on the job.[10] The workplace, therefore, is an important setting not only for health protection—to prevent occupational injury—but also for health promotion—to improve overall health and well-being.

Health promotion activities may include medical services, information, training, financial support, and promotional programs to enable and encourage workers to develop healthy lifestyle practices. Employers might:[11]

- Provide fitness facilities for workers or a financial subsidy for fitness classes or equipment.
- Encourage walking and cycling during work functions.
- Provide and subsidize healthy food choices in break rooms
- Allow flexibility in timing and length of work breaks to allow for exercise

Physical wellness influences other aspects of life. When people feel good physically, their intellectual, emotional, and spiritual connections strengthen.

In the post-COVID era, there are many digital resources available that can support wellness journeys. From YouTube workouts to community fitness groups, individuals can explore various options. As wellness advocates emphasize, the key is not necessarily the specific activity but the connection and engagement it fosters. Finding a supportive community or a personal trainer can enhance motivation and accountability, leading to a more fulfilling wellness experience.

Here is a short guide on how to do this in your office:[12]

- **Foster a Culture of Health:** Creating a culture of health is essential for successful physical activity programs. Dr. Nico Pronk defines a culture of health as an environment where individuals feel supported in their physical activity efforts, seamlessly integrating wellness into their daily routines without needing explicit approval from supervisors. This involves policies encouraging health and wellness. Research indicates that fitness center usage is often low and tends to attract already active individuals. Effective programs create lasting change by shaping organizational culture and inspiring employees to adopt healthier behaviors, with support from colleagues and managers.

- **Leaders Must Show Active Support:** Active and visible support from leaders is crucial for building a culture of health. It's not enough for high-level leaders to endorse wellness programs; middle managers play a significant role in daily operations and can unintentionally create barriers. Dr. Miriam Nelson notes that employees must witness their leaders actively participating in programs rather than simply giving permission. This sets a tone of commitment and engagement throughout the organization.

- **Leverage Community Partnerships:** According to Dr. Pronk, workplace health promotion efforts should extend beyond the office to include community resources and partnerships. Employees live in their communities, so businesses benefit from engaging with local leaders to reinforce healthy living messages. This is especially valuable for small businesses without the resources for fitness facilities. Collaborating with community groups can enhance neighborhood walkability and promote active transportation.

- o   Additionally, employers should foster social support networks within the workplace. Initiatives like walking clubs, physical activity contracts, and group exercises can help employees stay motivated, leading to increased physical activity and improved fitness.

- **Optimize Existing Resources:** Dr. Steven Blair points out that every workplace can improve its infrastructure to encourage physical activity. Simple changes like better lighting or signage in hallways and encouraging stair use can make a big difference. Dr. Greg Heath suggests that promoting active transportation—like walking or biking to work—can significantly boost physical activity levels at a low cost. Employers can collaborate with local governments to enhance the safety and appeal of the surrounding area.

- **Launch a Community-Wide Education Campaign:** Implementing an educational campaign can champion the benefits of physical activity and offer tools to overcome barriers. Campaigns should use clear, visible messages through various channels, such as meetings, emails, and newsletters, and include outreach activities like health screenings and educational workshops.

- **Tailor Programs to Employee Needs:** Dr. Nelson asserts that different people are motivated by different factors, so programming should be customized. Fitness apps motivate less active employees, while more active individuals might benefit from peer support. Research supports personalized health behavior programs focusing on individual needs, including skill-building in goal-setting and self-monitoring.

- **Address Multiple Factors for Greater Success:** To maximize success, it's important to target multiple factors. Dr. Nelson emphasizes that effective programs should build a comprehensive culture of health. They should also be socially and economically rewarding, relevant to employees, and aligned with the organization's culture.

- **Utilize Technology to Enhance Engagement:** According to Dr. Blair, modern technology can help reduce sedentary lifestyles. While new apps and devices show promise for promoting behavior change, their effects are still being studied. Employers should evaluate the impact of these technologies and share their findings.

- **Set Realistic Goals and Monitor Progress:** Dr. Mukhtar highlighted that continuous monitoring and evaluation are vital for achieving goals. This process helps identify areas for improvement, ensuring better programs and healthier employees. Establishing achievable goals based on employees' fitness levels is important, such as reducing sedentary time and progressing gradually. Organizational goals should also be realistic; for instance, aiming for 80% of managers to actively support a health promotion program within the first year can lay the groundwork for focusing on employee goals in subsequent years. Expectations should be adjusted according to the size and resources of the organization, as smaller businesses may face different challenges than larger corporations with dedicated wellness programs.

# Emotional Wellness

Marni was a bright and ambitious employee at a bustling marketing agency in her early twenties. Her energy was infectious, but her emotional well-being often fluctuated, particularly under pressure. One autumn afternoon, the team prepared for a crucial campaign launch that could make or break their quarter. As deadlines loomed, the atmosphere in the office became charged with anxiety.

Marni's coworker, Lisa, was known for her creativity and tendency to become overwhelmed. In the face of mounting stress, she struggled to manage her emotions. When faced with unexpected setbacks, such as last-minute changes from the client, Lisa often reacted with frustration. She would raise her voice during team meetings, expressing her discontent, which only added to the tension in the room. Observing this, Marni felt a mix of concern and frustration; she admired Lisa's talent but wished she could find a way to channel her emotions more constructively.

One day, during a particularly heated meeting, Lisa broke down. The pressure had become too much, and her tears caught everyone off guard. Instead of retreating into silence, something shifted within her. With the support of her colleagues, Lisa took a step back to reflect on her responses. That evening, she began to explore new strategies for coping with stress. She started journaling her thoughts, practicing mindfulness, and seeking feedback from her peers.

Over the following weeks, Lisa transformed her approach. In subsequent meetings, she practiced active listening, acknowledging her teammates' concerns before sharing her own. When challenges arose, she addressed them calmly and focused on solutions rather than problems. Her shift was not just noticeable; it was inspiring. Colleagues began to see Lisa as a source of support rather than stress.

Marni was particularly affected by this change. Witnessing Lisa's journey encouraged her to evaluate her emotional responses. She realized that while reacting negatively in stressful situations was easy, there was power in choosing a different path. Inspired by Lisa, Marni began implementing similar practices in her own life. She started each day with mindfulness, allowing herself to center her thoughts before diving into work.

As the campaign launch approached, the team became more cohesive, united by a shared commitment to positivity and resilience. When the project was finally unveiled, it was a resounding success. Lisa stood in front of the room, beaming with pride. She thanked her teammates for their support, acknowledging the journey they had all taken together. At that moment, Marni deeply admired Lisa—not just for her talent but for her ability to turn adversity into opportunity.

Through Lisa's transformation, Marni learned an invaluable lesson: **emotional well-being is a practice**, not a destination. How one responds to challenges can significantly influence the environment around them. Inspired by her coworker's growth, Marni embraced her emotional journey, striving to cultivate resilience and positivity in her workplace.

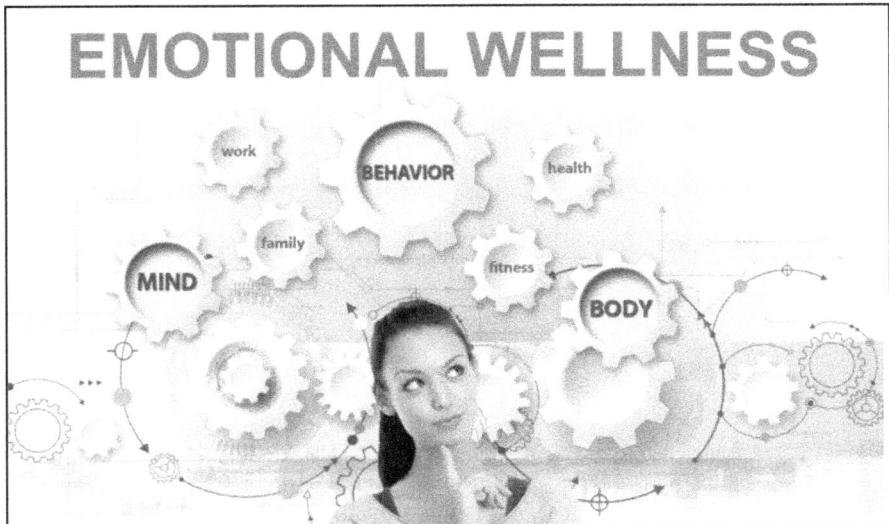

\* \* \*

Emotional well-being is managing our emotions while navigating daily life and work stresses. When we experience positive emotional well-being, we can approach challenging situations with an optimistic and proactive mindset, focusing on solutions. Conversely, when our emotional well-being is compromised, we may find it difficult to handle unexpected events, hesitate to address urgent issues and struggle to make effective decisions.

A 2021 Gallup report revealed that only 34% of Americans rated their emotional well-being as "excellent," marking a historic low. [13] Gallup also measures employee "engagement," which reflects how enthusiastic and committed staff are to their workplace. High engagement is linked to improved productivity, customer service, employee health, and overall well-being. Gallup research shows that a dedicated workforce can boost profitability by 21%.

Gallup emphasizes, *"Engagement and well-being are interconnected—each affects the other's future state. They provide unique but complementary benefits to employees' thoughts, feelings, behaviors, and performance. When aligned, they supercharge a thriving, productive workplace ... reducing burnout and enhancing productivity."*

Wow. 21%. As small business owners, we think about what a 21% boost to the bottom line can mean. Imagine what could happen if you added this component of wellness to your company...for your profitability alone!

## What We Say Matters

*"Whether you think you can or can't, you're right."*

The power of language is often underestimated—words reflect how one thinks, and thoughts are directly linked to belief systems. This highlights how individuals begin to recognize and express their feelings in healthy ways, using language to shape the world they want to create.

The connection between emotional wellness and a growth mindset is clear. When individuals dwell on the past or an imagined future, they lose awareness of their words and actions in the present moment. Talking about challenges is a key aspect of coping.

**PROTIP**: *"Between stimulus and response, there is a space. In that space, we have the power to choose our response. In our response lies our growth and our freedom."* - Viktor Frankl

Your power is always in this space. When you lose control of your emotions, you leak power. A good tip is to imagine filtering everything you say through your heart before it comes out of your mouth. Use the power of the pause to help you do this, especially when you feel yourself getting heated emotionally.

## Worthiness and Belonging

We have had many conversations with our clients about "imposter syndrome" and feelings of unworthiness.

Imposter syndrome is a psychological pattern where individuals doubt their abilities, accomplishments, or intelligence and fear being exposed as a fraud, even when there's clear evidence of their competence.

People with imposter syndrome often attribute their success to luck or something similar rather than their own skills, and they may feel they don't deserve recognition. This can lead to self-doubt, perfectionism, and anxiety despite achieving high levels of success. It's common in high achievers and can affect anyone, regardless of your career, background, or level of expertise. Recognizing and addressing these feelings can help build confidence and self-worth.

We must recognize that worthiness is something we actively decide for ourselves. Our emotional wellness is deeply connected to our feelings of worthiness and belonging. Our self-worth can quickly derail when imposter syndrome creeps in. Feelings of unworthiness are often a symptom of low self-esteem. As self-esteem improves, individuals regulate their behavior to align with their values, leading to greater emotional wellness. [14]

Core values are personal ethics or ideals that guide you when making decisions, building relationships, and solving problems. Identifying the values that are meaningful to you can help you develop and achieve personal and professional goals.

It took Marni years to realize the importance of identifying her core values, especially when working with clients whose values did not align with hers. This also applies to personal and professional relationships. Core values are at the heart of everything we do. Identifying our core values is paramount to ensuring we match them and align them with our professional lives.

When people's values are misaligned, it can lead to a disconnect in behavior and self-worth. By identifying and staying true to core values, individuals can practice self-compassion and cope better with feelings of unworthiness. For Marni, integrity, compassion, vulnerability with healthy boundaries, growth, and servant leadership are key values that guide their work. For Tiffany, it's all about operating with integrity, compassion, empathy, absolute support, servant leadership and kindness.

## Emotional Wellness Broken Down

This section will reference four categories you can incorporate into emotional wellness.[15]

- Build Resilience
- Reduce Stress
- Get Quality Sleep
- Be Mindful

## Building Resilience

Dr. Cindy Bergman, a psychology professor at the University of Notre Dame, says, *"Resilience is the extent to which we can bounce back from adverse events, cope with stress, or succeed in the face of adversity."*[16]

Everyone experiences tough times. How we navigate stress sets people apart—some merely survive, while others thrive. Like many things, building resilience is a journey, and there is no one-size-fits-all approach.

The National Institute of Health suggests a few key strategies, such as developing healthy physical habits and taking time for self-care. For instance, recognizing when the body needs rest is essential. After feeling physically exhausted, indulging in a favorite meal, relaxing, meditating, or simply decompressing is crucial. Other recommendations include viewing problems from different perspectives and seeing challenges as growth opportunities.

Gratitude also plays a significant role in resilience. It is a powerful tool to overcome fear, often ego-driven. In stressful situations, practicing gratitude can shift one's mindset.

Marni often recalls her early twenties, when she was a spokesperson for a network marketing company, traveling across the country to speak in front of huge crowds. Public speaking always made her nervous. "I wasn't sure how I learned to handle it," she says, "but I developed a ritual that I still use from a very young age. Before stepping on stage, I would find a bathroom and go in there to center myself."

When the fear started to rise, Marni would turn to gratitude. "I'd focus on everything I was thankful for—getting out of bed that morning, the fact that I have two feet to touch the floor, my healthy body that allowed me to be there, the car that brought me safely to the venue, and the people who had traveled to hear me speak. I'd even be grateful for the exact words to help me connect with them."

Over the years, she's learned that gratitude is one of the most powerful tools in our arsenal, a way to shift fear into confidence. It's also recognizing our "ego self," or lower self, when it shows up. It's what Marni likes to call the "inner mean girl/guy." The voice that says you aren't good enough. How do you overcome that? Gratitude! For Marni, it remains a grounding practice, and she believes that practicing gratitude is crucial for navigating challenges and maintaining resilience.

Resilience can be supported by exploring one's beliefs about the meaning and purpose of life, tapping into social connections, and seeking help when necessary. Mental health resources, including licensed counselors, are more available than ever, especially post-pandemic. **Mental health *is* health**; seeking support is vital to managing stress and building resilience.

\* \* \* \*

Julia, a driven woman in her thirties, had worked as a project manager for a mid-sized tech company for the past five years. She was known for her attention to detail and ability to juggle multiple tasks. Still, when a high-profile client began to unravel, her resilience would be tested like never before.

The large retail chain client had invested heavily in Julia's company's software and was expecting a smooth rollout. However, on launch day, the system crashed. Emails flooded in, and the phone rang nonstop as frustrated users reported the issue. Julia, overwhelmed, felt the weight of the company's reputation on her shoulders.

Her first instinct was panic. How could this happen on her watch? But after a deep breath, she shifted gears. She gathered her team and created a game plan to solve the issue while keeping communication clear and constant. Julia spoke with the client directly, apologizing for the inconvenience and promising swift action. She remained calm and empathetic, even as the client's tone grew harsher.

For three straight days, Julia and her team worked around the clock. She met each setback with new solutions and kept her focus. She realized that resilience wasn't just about enduring; it was about adapting, learning from each challenge, and staying centered under pressure.

Ultimately, the problem was resolved, and the client—impressed by Julia's composure and commitment—renewed their contract. Julia had not only saved the day but also discovered her strength in the process.

Nurturing your body, brain, and social connections can help you recover from stress.

## Checklist for Building Emotional Wellness[17]

- **Develop healthy physical habits.** Healthy eating, physical activity, and regular sleep can improve physical and mental health.

- **Take time for yourself.** Make taking care of yourself part of your daily routine. Take time to notice the good moments or do something you enjoy, like reading a book or listening to music.

- **Look at problems from different angles.** Think of challenging situations as growth opportunities. Try to see the positive side of things. Learn from your mistakes, and don't dwell on them.

- **Practice gratitude.** Take time to note things to be thankful for each day.

- **Explore your beliefs about the meaning and purpose of life.** Think about how to guide your life by the principles that are important to you.

- **Tap into your social connections and community.** Surround yourself with positive, healthy people. Ask friends, family, or trusted community members for information or assistance when needed. Look for cultural practices that you feel help in times of stress.

- **Get help for mental health and substance use disorders.** Talk with a healthcare professional if you're having trouble coping. Or call SAMHSA's free national helpline at 1-800-662-HELP. If you or someone you know is thinking about suicide, you can call the National Suicide Prevention Lifeline at 1-800-273-TALK. You can also text "HOME" to the Crisis Text Line at 741741.

## Reducing Stress

Everyone experiences stress from time to time. It's a natural reaction to challenges or demands. Stress can stem from daily pressures at work or home. However, it's more than just feeling busy, explains Dr. Janice Kiecolt-Glaser from Ohio State University, who researches the impact of stress on the body.[18]

"Stress is the feeling of being overloaded, out of control, and unable to cope," she says.

Stress can also arise from sudden life changes, like a divorce or job loss. Traumatic events, such as accidents, assaults, or natural disasters, can lead to severe stress.

Learning to manage stress is crucial for maintaining your health and well-being. Researchers continue to explore how stress impacts the body and are developing techniques to help people feel calmer and more relaxed.

Marni often reflects on her many years of therapy, which began when she was just twelve years old. Now, at forty-four years old, after countless sessions, one of the most valuable lessons she's learned is **the nature of overwhelm**. She explains that overwhelm results from feeling too many emotions simultaneously—fear, anger, frustration, anxiety, and sometimes even joy. This stress makes it difficult for the brain to function. The experience of overwhelm is not just about feeling one emotion intensely; it's the confusion that comes from juggling so many emotions simultaneously.

To help manage stress, Marni emphasizes becoming **an observer of your own emotions**. She often shares this with her clients, encouraging them to visualize their higher self, or soul self, as though it's hovering above them, looking down without judgment.

The lower mind and higher mind represent two levels of thinking. The lower mind is tied to ego, fear, and reactive thought patterns, often driven by survival instincts and external validation. The higher mind, on the other hand, is connected to intuition, wisdom, and clarity, guiding you toward truth and higher purpose.

You are not your mind; instead, your mind is a tool you can use to process and create. You can recognize this by observing your thoughts without attachment—when you notice that you can watch your mind at work, it becomes clear that you are the observer, not the thinker. This awareness allows you to step out of mental chatter and consciously choose thoughts aligned with your higher self.

The practice of non-judgmental observation is key to building self-awareness. Instead of asking, "What's wrong with me?" or "Why do I feel this way?" Marni suggests shifting to a more neutral perspective: "Isn't it interesting that I've been feeling angry lately?" or "I notice I'm feeling overwhelmed.". She believes gaining the clarity needed to address and resolve emotional challenges is impossible without it. Advocating for yourself begins with recognizing your feelings from this detached, insightful stance.

Tiffany reflects on how stress is often more than just being busy. "Stress isn't just about having a packed schedule," she explains. "It's the feeling of being overloaded, out of control, and unable to cope; that's when things can spiral." She points out that losing the ability to cope can lead to a deeper sense of overwhelm. However, Tiffany emphasizes the importance of self-awareness, echoing Marni's advice about observing yourself without judgment or emotion. This allows you to calmly recognize what's happening and how you're reacting, making it easier to manage the situation.

Tiffany acknowledges that life's major stressors—like a loved one falling ill or experiencing a natural disaster—can create severe stress. However, we can better navigate these challenges by recognizing those changes and understanding that we have the tools to handle them. She stresses the importance of being observant of the signs of stress and excessive stress, particularly emotions like anger or irritability. Once we recognize those signs, we can take action to address them.

Drawing from NIH guidelines, Tiffany highlights how regular exercise has a profound positive effect on the body and mind. "Even something as simple as going for a walk is powerful," she says. One day that was particularly stressful, she'd had a few client-related issues and decided to pause and take her mom to lunch. This simple break provided her with a reset. When she returned to her client's health promotion and meetings in the afternoon, her performance and mindset had improved dramatically. Tiffany believes that her self-awareness and decision to take a break allowed her to handle challenges more effectively.

She also emphasizes scheduling regular relaxation activities, referencing mindfulness, breathing exercises, and meditation as key tools. For her, even something as simple as watching a meditation video or viewing calming photos online can recharge and re-energize her. "Gratitude plays a huge role in this process, too," Tiffany adds, noting how impactful these moments of reflection can be in resetting her energy and outlook. By taking the time to pause and be self-aware, she feels more equipped to handle the demands of everyday life.

**Feeling Overwhelmed? Learn to Manage Stress. Here are some ways to do that:**[19]

- *Be observant.* Recognize signs of excessive stress. These include difficulty sleeping, being easily angered or irritable, feeling depressed, and low energy.

- *Exercise regularly.* 10-20 minutes per day of walking can help boost your mood and reduce stress.

- *Schedule regular times for a relaxing activity.* Activities that use mindfulness or breathing exercises, such as meditation, yoga, or tai chi, may help.

- *Get enough sleep.* Adults need about seven or more hours of sleep per night. School-age children need 9–12 hours, while teenagers need 8–10 hours.

- *Set goals and priorities.* Decide what must get done now and what can wait. Learn to say "no" to new tasks if you take on too much.

- *Build a social support network.* Stay connected with people who can provide emotional support.

- *Show compassion for yourself.* Note what you've accomplished at the end of the day, not what you've failed to do.

- *Seek help.* Talk to a health care provider if you feel unable to cope, have suicidal thoughts, or use drugs or alcohol to cope. If you or someone you know is in crisis, call the National Suicide Prevention Lifeline at 1-800-273-TALK (8255). Or text "HOME" to the Crisis Text Line at 741741.

## Getting Quality Sleep

Finding time to pause and rest can feel impossible in today's fast-paced world. A full night of quality sleep seems out of reach sometimes. However, sleep is as vital to your health as proper diet and exercise. A good night's rest boosts brain function, improves mood, and supports overall well-being. Consistently missing out on quality sleep can increase the risk of heart disease, stroke, obesity, and even dementia.

Tiffany knows firsthand the importance of quality sleep and has had conversations with her clients about this. She recalls a conversation with her friend Tina, who thought she could just "catch up" on her days off on her sleep. Researchers are finding that this largely isn't the case.[20]

*"If you have one bad night's sleep and take a nap or sleep longer the next night, that can benefit you,"* says Dr. Kenneth Wright, Jr., a sleep researcher at the University of Colorado. *"But if you have a week's worth of getting too little sleep, the weekend isn't sufficient for you to catch up. That's not healthy behavior."*

In a recent study, Wright and his team looked at people with consistently deficient sleep. They compared them to sleep-deprived people who got to sleep in on the weekend. Both groups of people gained weight due to lack of sleep. Their bodies' ability to control blood sugar levels also got worse. The weekend catch-up sleep didn't help. But more sleep isn't always better, says Dr. Wright. *"If you're sleeping more than nine hours a night and you still don't feel refreshed, there may be some underlying medical issue,"* she explains.

Why do we need sleep? Many people view it simply as "downtime" for a weary brain. Dr. Maiken Nedergaard, a sleep researcher at the University of Rochester, emphasizes that this perception is misleading.

"*While you sleep, your brain is actively working,*" she explains. Sleep is crucial in preparing the brain for learning, memory, and creativity.[21]

Nedergaard and her team discovered that the brain has a drainage system that removes toxins during sleep. "*When we sleep, the brain undergoes significant changes in function,*" she notes, comparing it to a kidney that filters waste from the system.

Her research with mice showed that this drainage system eliminates proteins associated with Alzheimer's disease at twice the rate it does during sleep.

Dr. Wright adds that sleep is essential for the body's repair processes. "*Certain restorative functions occur most effectively during sleep,*" he states. "*Those vital processes are disrupted if you don't sleep enough.*"

**Getting a Better Night's Sleep[22]**

- *Stick to a sleep schedule.* Go to bed and wake up at the same time every day, even on the weekends.
- *Get some exercise every day.* But not too close to bedtime.
- *Go outside.* Try to get natural sunlight for at least 30 minutes every day.
- *Avoid nicotine and caffeine.* Both are stimulants that keep you awake; caffeine can take 6–8 hours to wear off completely.
- *Limit napping.* Don't take naps after mid-afternoon. Keep all naps short.
- *Avoid alcohol and large meals before bedtime.* Both can prevent deep, restorative sleep.
- *Limit electronics before bed.* Instead, try reading a book, listening to soothing music, or doing another relaxing activity.

- *Create a good sleeping environment.* If possible, keep the temperature cool. Remove sound and light distractions. Make it dark. Silence your cell phone.
- *Don't lie in bed awake.* If you can't fall asleep after twenty minutes, get up and do a relaxing activity until you feel sleepy again.
- *See your healthcare provider.* If nothing you try helps, they can determine if you need further testing. They can also help you learn new ways to manage stress.

## Be Mindful

Mindfulness is an incredible tool for improving emotional wellness. It is the quality or state of being conscious or aware of something. The more awareness we bring to our everyday lives, the more control we have.

When Marni started working with a client, Dr. Smith, an orthodontist, she noted that a particular employee had difficulty managing her emotions.

Tina was a treatment coordinator and a high producer. She could close high-dollar cases. But her emotional struggles took a toll. Marni gave her a beginner's guide to mindfulness book to start working on regulating her emotions. After a week, Tina began shifting into a more growth mindset. She wanted to be better but needed more resources and tools. Marni worked with her for months and Tina's work rubbed off on the other team members. Marni ended up helping that practice by having a 6-week mindfulness course that the team did together as a group. This was a huge culture boost and really helped solidify the tools the team needed. The beginning tool she teaches is the idea of *learning to be present.*

Mindfulness begins with *being present;* if you are not living in the present, you cannot bring awareness to your world. Being present means focusing on today, not living in the past or an imagined future. In this way, the present moment becomes a gift. That's why it's called the "present." We can use many tools to help us keep in the present.

Here are some tools to help you remember to stay present:

1. **Deep Breathing**
   o Breath is constant. It's one of the best tools we can use to help us to come into the here and now. Practice slow, intentional breaths to anchor yourself in the moment.
2. **Body Scan Meditation**
   o Bring awareness to each part of your body, noticing sensations without judgment.
3. **Mindful Observation**
   o Focus on one object, noticing its details like color, texture, and shape.

4.  **Gratitude Practice**
    o   Pause to reflect on three things you're grateful for in the present moment.

5.  **Grounding Exercises**
    o   Use the "5-4-3-2-1" technique to engage your senses: name 5 things you see, 4 you hear, 3 you feel, 2 you smell, and 1 you taste.

6.  **Mindful Walking**
    o   Pay attention to the sensation of your feet touching the ground as you walk.

7.  **Set Daily Intentions**
    o   Start your day with a mindful affirmation, like "I will focus on the present."

8.  **Mindfulness Apps**
    o   Use apps like Headspace or Insight Timer for guided practices.

9.  **Alarms or Sticky Notes**
    o   Set reminders on your phone or place notes around your space with phrases like "Be here now."

10. **Journaling**
    o   Write down your thoughts to process them and refocus on the present.

11. **Mindful Listening**
    o   Fully engage when someone speaks, focusing on their words without planning your response.

12. **Pause and Check-In**
    o   Throughout the day, pause to ask yourself: "What am I thinking or feeling right now?"

Once you learn to be present, you will start developing awareness. Marni encourages team members to imagine watching themselves from outside. Marni also encourages the use of curiosity as a tool. It is a powerful tool for developing awareness of mindfulness, as it encourages an open, nonjudgmental approach to your thoughts, emotions, and experiences.

Instead of reacting to challenges or distractions, you can pause and ask, "What is happening right now?" or "Why do I feel this way?" This gentle questioning invites you to explore your inner world with interest rather than criticism. For example, when a difficult emotion arises, curiosity helps you examine its source, physical sensations, and triggers without attaching labels like "good" or "bad." By staying curious, you cultivate a beginner's mindset, seeing each moment as fresh and full of potential, which deepens your awareness and allows you to respond more thoughtfully to life's situations.

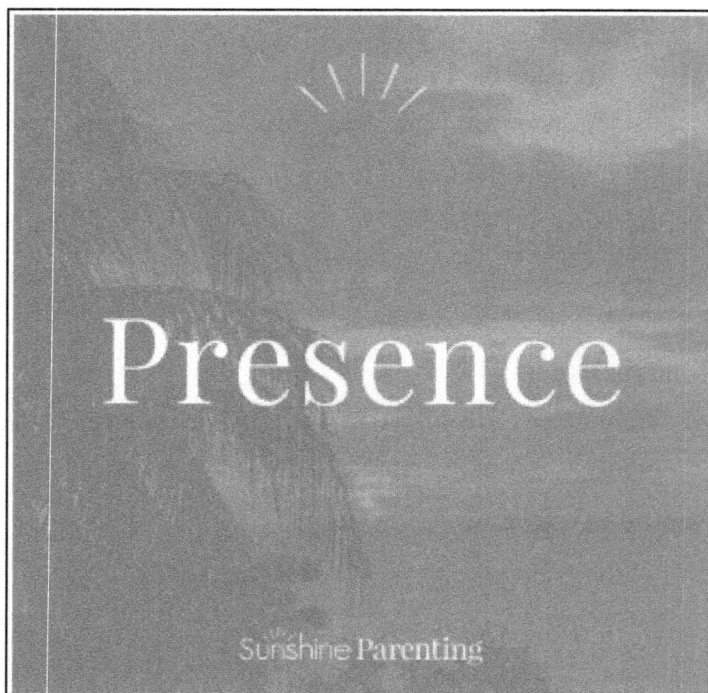

Presence

Sunshine Parenting

## The Health Benefits of Mindfulness

Research indicates that being present in the moment can positively impact both mental and physical health. Mindfulness-based practices may alleviate anxiety and depression, lower blood pressure, and improve sleep quality. Additionally, mindfulness may assist in managing pain. "For many chronic conditions, mindfulness meditation seems to enhance the quality of life and lessen mental health symptoms," says Dr. Zev Schuman-Olivier of Harvard University.[23]

Dr. Sona Dimidjian of the University of Colorado Boulder explains that mindfulness fights depression in two ways. First, it anchors your attention to the present moment. Second, mindfulness fosters "de-centering" from distressing thoughts. Dimidjian explains. "This skill helps you avoid getting swept away by thoughts like, 'Nothing ever works out for me,' or 'Things will always be this way.' With practice, you can learn to step back from these painful thought patterns."

Researchers are now exploring whether mindfulness training can benefit other conditions, including PTSD, eating disorders, and addiction. Becoming more mindful requires practice. Here are some additional mindfulness tips to help you get started:

- **Try Breathwork.** If you simply google "breathwork techniques," you will find so many simple things to do! This can be great for relieving anxiety in a quick way. Bonus tip – if you are working with a patient or customer who is having anxiety, you can teach them how to do this breathwork and you both benefit.

**Alternate Nostril Breathing**

Sit comfortably with a straight spine. Rest your left hand in your lap and fold the index and middle fingers down, leaving the thumb, ring, and pinky fingers extended.

1. **Close the Right Nostril**: Use the thumb to gently close the right nostril and inhale deeply through the left nostril.
2. **Close the Left Nostril**: Use the ring finger to close the left nostril, release the thumb, and exhale through the right nostril.
3. **Inhale Through the Right Nostril**: Breathe deeply through the right nostril.
4. **Switch and Exhale Through the Left Nostril**: Close the right nostril again and exhale through the left.

This completes one cycle. Repeat 5–10 cycles, breathing slowly and evenly. Stay relaxed and focus on the breath to promote balance and calm.

- **Enjoy a stroll.** Pay attention to your breath and the sights and sounds around you as you walk. If thoughts and worries enter your mind, note them and then return to the present.
- **Practice mindful eating.** Be aware of taste, textures, and flavors in each bite. Listen to your body when it is hungry or full.

# Spiritual Wellness

Francesca, a vibrant woman in her thirties, believed that hard work and hustle were the keys to success. She poured every ounce of energy into building a small boutique marketing agency she co-owned. Late nights, early mornings, and constant problem-solving became her norm. Despite a growing list of clients and accolades, Francesca felt something was missing.

She noticed it most on a Tuesday afternoon when her stress peaked. A major client unexpectedly pulled out, and Francesca felt emotionally and physically drained in the chaos of trying to recover. No amount of caffeine or a "power through" mindset could fix what she felt—an emptiness that success alone couldn't fill.

After working with Francesca, we realized that she needed spiritual balance. We encouraged her to adopt this in her life. Ironically, her friend invited her to a wellness retreat focused on spiritual balance. Reluctantly, Francesca agreed to go, more out of curiosity than conviction. There, amid peaceful surroundings and moments of silence, Francesca learned of spiritual wellness: aligning one's inner self with one's outer actions.

During a meditation session, Francesca realized she had been neglecting her inner world for years. She had focused solely on achieving external success and overlooked her emotional and spiritual well-being.

At the retreat, the leaders discussed how spiritual wellness leads to self-awareness, mindfulness, and a deeper connection to purpose, not religion.

At that moment, Francesca saw how disconnected she had become. She was chasing professional goals without nurturing her spirit. So, she began practicing mindfulness daily and grounding herself in gratitude.

As Francesca embraced spiritual wellness, her career changed. She was more present with her clients, more creative, and less reactive to stressful situations. Her team noticed that her calm energy influenced how they handled challenges, and the workplace became more balanced.

Francesca's business continued to grow, but this time, success felt different. It wasn't just about the numbers or the next big client. It was about *alignment*—between her inner peace and her professional life. She had learned that true success wasn't just what she achieved but how she felt.

Spiritual wellness means different things to different people, but it's ultimately about our relationship with ourselves, our connection to humanity, and how we fit into the bigger picture.

## Signs of Spiritual Wellness[24]

- Developing a purpose in life
- Having the ability to spend reflective time alone
- Taking time to reflect on the meaning of events in life
- Having a clear sense of right and wrong and acting accordingly
- Having the ability to explain why you believe what you believe
- Caring and acting for the welfare of others and the environment
- Being able to practice forgiveness and compassion in life

## Spiritual Wellness Goes Beyond Religion

Connection and belonging are why we are here. We are hardwired for this. It's often taboo to talk about spirituality in business and for Marni, she is just learning to come out of her spiritual "closet." She hasn't wanted to talk about it in a business setting because it can be divisive, which is not the intention of the discussion.

In the context of what we are discussing here, this is not about religion or worship; it's a resource for everyone, regardless of belief, to explore how we're all connected and discover ways to cultivate inner peace, love, and stronger relationships in our communities. For some, the bigger picture is God, the universe, or a higher power. No matter; it's something beyond what we experience daily. Bringing this larger sense of connection and belonging to our teams is a wonderful practice. What we are really talking about here is finding your own individualized purpose.

Understanding what gives your life meaning and how that aligns with your values. Practices like forgiveness, both of yourself and others, self-reflection, and spending time in nature can deepen this connection to your inner self. Journaling is another tool that can help you reflect on who you are and what you want to project into the world.

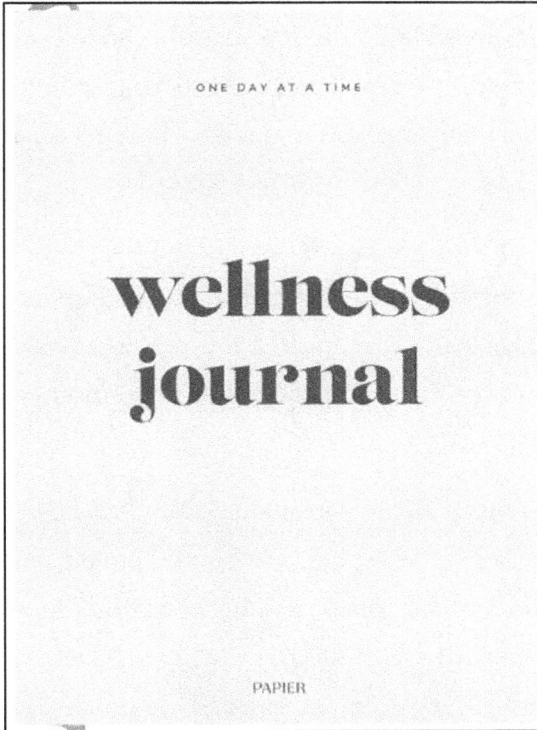

ONE DAY AT A TIME

# wellness journal

PAPIER

It starts with exploring your spiritual core by asking, "Who am I? What is my purpose? What do I value most?" These questions can guide you toward fulfillment. This process is part of finding deeper meaning in life, recognizing patterns, and knowing what we can control. Practices like yoga, meditation, positive thinking, and self-reflection are tools that can also help you foster spiritual wellness.

It's also important to broaden your mind and consider different perspectives, which can help you experience a greater sense of purpose. Personal growth often comes from embracing challenges and cultivating a strengths-focused mindset. **CliftonStrengths**, for example, is an excellent tool for identifying and building on your strengths, giving you the confidence to pursue your purpose.

**Purpose** is like an invisible compass that guides you toward fulfillment. It's an evolving journey. Life experiences can spark inspiration and lead you down new paths. Your purpose today may not be the same as it was 25 years ago, and that's okay. It's about growth and self-discovery.

Surround yourself with a supportive community or "tribe" of people who see and nurture your potential. Sometimes, others can help you see things you hadn't recognized in yourself. This feedback can be a powerful motivator, encouraging you to pursue new opportunities that align with your strengths.

Spiritual wellness is a deeply personal journey that helps us explore our connection to ourselves, others, and the world around us. It's about finding meaning, cultivating inner peace, and understanding how we fit into the bigger picture. Spiritual wellness is not a religion. Instead, it's an invitation to engage in self-discovery, compassion, and mindful living.

## Exercises to Foster Spiritual Wellness

### 1. Explore Your Spiritual Core with Self-Inquiry:

Here are some powerful exercises that may assist you in the journey inside. As you do these, please take a moment at the start to center yourself and get into a deeper awareness and ask your intuitive guidance to answer these questions with you. We are able to see more clearly when we come from a deeper consciousness or state of awareness, so by taking the time to settle into that space first, the information may flow out of you from that deep well of inner knowing. Take your time with this; there is a lot here. Each line item may be something you journal about each day.

Begin by asking powerful questions that invite you to explore your deeper self.

**Exercise in becoming more aware of my energy management** (Credit to Nancy Burns)

- Am I completely anchored here in the present time?
- If not, what is keeping me fractured and not fully present? (unfinished business, unforgiveness, unworthiness, too much to do)
- Where is my energy going?
- Where is my power?
- What has me distracted and what is consuming my thoughts?
- Has a lack of being in the present time (which is the only place to create from) affected my physical wellness?
- Is my energy being drained?
- What is draining that energy? (relationships, habits, work, home life, lack of organization or focus)
- How do I get the energy back?
- How do I empower myself?
- Am I losing energy by trying to control another?
- Am I losing energy because I am worrying about another?
- Am I imposing my energy on another or being drained by another stronger or needier personality?

**Exercise in becoming aware of core beliefs:**

- List the things that you feel you SHOULD do. (or feel a sense of responsibility for)
- Ask yourself WHY you should do them.
- Ask yourself WHO you are doing them for.
- Notice the energetic response of the body for each one. Does it feel good, empower you, drain you? Connect the response to a part of the body, if possible.

**Exercise in becoming aware of how you may be subconsciously controlling your life:**

- Do you have repetitive patterns for distraction?
- Do self-conscious thoughts keep you from being who you are or from expressing yourself fully?
- Do limiting thoughts keep you from fully participating? (money, health, fear of rejection)
- Look for repetitive habits that are substitutes for controlling your will. (they may be showing up as physical pain)
- Uncover any repetitive patterns of failure that may have a hold on you.
- What are your fear patterns?

**Exercise to awaken the conscious self.**

- What do I like?
- What do I love?
- What don't I love?
- What makes me happy?
- What do I need in my life for balance?
- What are my strengths?

— What are my weaknesses?

— Can I rely on myself?

— How do I undermine myself?

— Why do I do the things I do? What motivates me?

— What makes me need the attention and approval of others?

— Am I strong enough to be close to another and still honor my own emotional needs?

— What possible changes would I be willing to make to heal? (relationships, diet, exercise, work, face fears)

— Notice the different choices between the heart and the mind. Who do I love in my heart? Who do I love in my mind? Are they in sync?

**Exercise to identify your core spiritual values:**

— At the end of your life, what will the three most important lessons be and why?

— Who do you most deeply respect and why? List their qualities.

— Who are you at your best?

— Does your life fully reflect your authentic self? If not, where is it not in alignment with your true self?

— Do you love bravely? Or safely? Do you need to be loved back by someone you love?

— Does your life look like you want it to? Relationships? Work? Spiritual practice? Love? Friendships? Prosperity?

Mastery of the physical isn't the goal of becoming conscious; mastery of the spirit is the goal. The body follows. Marni's goal for you is to fall deeply in love with yourself again. Remember who you are and what you love, and live life to the fullest. Have fun with this, and may this work assist you in the journey into your heart!

## 2. Cultivate Awareness through Meditation

Meditation helps quiet the mind and create space for clarity and connection.

Exercise: Try a 10-minute guided meditation focused on breath awareness or body scanning. Apps like Calm, Insight Timer, or Headspace offer beginner-friendly sessions.

**Try this meditation:** (Heart/rose meditation by Nancy Burns)

- Breathe deeply
- Bring awareness to the heart
- Picture a fleshy red heart
- Compare heart to rosebud (pure, innocent, trusting)
- Imagine a rosebud blossoming and unfurling its petals
- Open to receive all the love and gratitude of the universe
- Share that love and gratitude
- Stay in that place for a while
- Feel your heart opening
- Tap into your heart regularly during the day

Reflection: After the meditation, write down how you feel and any insights that came to you. Notice if you feel more grounded or at peace.

## 3. Embrace Nature as a Spiritual Practice

Being in nature can bring a sense of awe, connectedness, and mindfulness.

Exercise: Plan a "nature walk" at least once a week. Find a quiet place—a park, beach, or hiking trail—and walk silently, focusing on your surroundings.

Reflection: After your walk, journal about the experience. What did you notice about yourself, your surroundings, and your emotions? How did being in nature affect your sense of connection?

## 4. Practice Forgiveness

Forgiveness is a cornerstone of spiritual wellness. It frees you from the burden of resentment and opens up space for healing.

Exercise: Write a letter of forgiveness to yourself or someone else. You don't have to send it, but express how you feel and what you are ready to release.

Reflection: How does forgiving yourself or others change how you view your purpose or relationships?

## 5. Create a Mindful Life Map

A life map can help visualize your spiritual journey and uncover key experiences that have shaped who you are today.

Exercise: Draw a timeline of your life, marking key events (both positive and challenging) that have impacted your spiritual growth. Include lessons learned, strengths developed, and how each phase contributed to your current purpose.

Reflection: What patterns do you notice? How have your values evolved, and how might they continue to evolve?

## 6. Write a Personal Mission Statement

Crafting a mission statement can provide clarity on your purpose and values.

Exercise: Write a personal mission statement by completing these prompts:

My purpose is to...

The values I strive to live by are...

I aim to contribute to the world by...

Review your mission statement regularly to keep it aligned with your evolving journey.

### 7. Broaden Your Perspective with New Experiences

Personal growth comes from being open to new ideas and perspectives.

Exercise: Listen to a podcast or read a book from a spiritual tradition or belief system you are unfamiliar with. Alternatively, attend a lecture or talk that challenges your thinking.

Reflection: How did this new perspective influence your understanding of yourself or your purpose? What insights can you apply to your life?

### 8. Discover Strengths with CliftonStrengths

Understanding your strengths can give you confidence in pursuing your purpose.

Exercise: Identify your strengths using the CliftonStrengths assessment (or a similar tool). Reflect on how these strengths appear in your daily life and align with your sense of purpose.

Reflection: How can you leverage your strengths to create more meaning and fulfillment?

### 9. Volunteer or Engage in Service

Serving others can deepen your connection to the world and enhance spiritual fulfillment.

Exercise: Volunteer for a cause that resonates with your values, whether at a local charity, community event, or through mentoring.

Reflection: After volunteering, consider how the experience made you feel. What did you learn about yourself and your sense of purpose through service?

### 10. Draft a Time-Travel Letter

Reflecting on your past, present, and future can bring clarity and insight into your spiritual journey.

Exercise: Write a letter to your past, present, and future self. Address what you've learned, where you are now, and where you hope to be.

Reflection: After writing the letters, contemplate how your journey has unfolded and what steps you can take to align more fully with your purpose.

Your spiritual wellness is not a destination; it's a lifelong journey of discovery and growth. By practicing self-reflection, embracing challenges, and surrounding yourself with supportive communities, you create the conditions for deepening your connection with yourself and the world. Remember, your purpose is not static; it evolves as you grow. When you engage in these exercises regularly, trust the process of uncovering meaning, inner peace, and fulfillment.

# Occupational Wellness

John, a seasoned businessman in his sixties, had owned a small manufacturing company for over three decades. We started working with him, and he shared with us that his business had always been steady, but in recent years, he noticed a dip in productivity and morale among his employees. It wasn't drastic, but enough for John to feel that something wasn't quite right. Turnover rates were increasing, and the team seemed to be going through the motions rather than thriving.

John, a man of routine and tradition, had never considered employee wellness beyond the basics. His philosophy had always been straightforward: pay fair wages, provide good benefits, and people will stay. However, during one of the leadership seminars he attended, we introduced the concept of occupational wellness—the idea that employees need more than just a paycheck; they need purpose, balance, and a sense of fulfillment in their work.

John decided to learn more. He embraced a growth mindset and started to understand that occupational wellness focuses on creating a work environment where people felt valued, had growth opportunities, and could balance work with their personal lives. He also understood that this way of thinking encourages employees to align their roles with their strengths and passions, fostering job satisfaction and productivity.

John realized his team had been operating on autopilot for too long. **He introduced some simple principles of occupational wellness:**

- Offering more flexibility with work hours and encouraging employees to take time off without guilt.

- Organizing short workshops to help employees identify their strengths and interests, encouraging them to take on tasks that excited them.
- Implementing "wellness check-ins" during weekly meetings, where the team could openly discuss challenges, suggest improvements, and celebrate small victories.

At first, some of the employees were skeptical. But slowly, John noticed the atmosphere shifting. People began collaborating and taking ownership of their roles. Sue, one of his longest-standing employees, had been on the verge of burnout. She found new energy when she took on a passion project—redesigning the company's sustainability efforts. Another employee, Mike, whose talent for leadership had gone unnoticed, was promoted to lead a new initiative after John saw his potential during a strengths assessment.

Within six months, John's business thrived in unexpected ways. Productivity skyrocketed, but more importantly, employees seemed genuinely happier. Turnover rates dropped, and John received unsolicited feedback from clients who noticed his team's engagement and enthusiasm.

By investing in occupational wellness, John created not just a more efficient workplace but a more vibrant one. His small business, once operating on tradition and routine, was now a place of growth and purpose—where both he and his team found fulfillment in the work they did each day.

## Achieving Occupational Wellness

Occupational wellness involves maintaining a healthy balance between work and leisure, leading to personal fulfillment, well-being, and financial stability. It reflects a state where individuals feel content and satisfied with their professional and personal lives.

People achieve occupational wellness when they do what they truly enjoy and find harmony between their careers and leisure time. This balance positively influences their work performance, interactions with others, and overall success in life.

## Signs of Occupational Wellness: [25]

- Engaging in meaningful and motivating work
- Balancing work with personal time for rest and recreation
- Working in a way that suits your learning style and preferences
- Communicating and collaborating effectively with colleagues

- Successfully working both independently and as part of a team
- Feeling inspired and challenged in your role
- Ending the day with a sense of accomplishment

## Tips for Improving Occupational Wellness:

- Stay motivated and continue working towards your career goals
- Build knowledge and skills to advance in your profession
- Focus on the positives and benefits of your current job
- Align your work with your passions and interests
- Foster strong connections with your colleagues
- Set clear goals, develop a plan, and take action to achieve them
- If you're feeling unfulfilled, consider seeking new opportunities or talking to a career counselor for guidance

# Intellectual Wellness

Tiffany recalls her time as a dental hygienist when she worked for a very insightful and observant doctor who was highly attuned to his team's needs. He was such a focused leader that he could tell when a team member needed a new challenge or opportunity. She distinctly recalls the day he said, 'I need to send you to another course.'

She was taken aback and asked, 'What do you mean? Where is this coming from?' He simply replied, 'You're getting bored.' She immediately questioned herself: ' Am I coming across as bored? Am I behaving in a certain way I'm not aware of?' Instead of seeing it as a positive opportunity, She initially questioned her professionalism."

She paused and realized, "He wasn't criticizing me. He was elevating me, seeing potential in me that I hadn't recognized myself. He put me in a leadership role, encouraging my personal and professional growth."

Working in an environment where leadership actively supports and nurtures the team is powerful. "When leaders come to us and say, 'I see you're ready for more,' it creates a full-circle effect within the company. By investing in team members through education, training, and coaching, people grow, and the company moves to a higher level. It's a continuous process of development and renewal. Age, background, or where someone grew up doesn't matter—everyone benefits from this support."

## Developing Mental Stimulation is a Key Growth Motivation Tool

Intellectual well-being is the idea of being involved in creative and mentally stimulating activities to pursue lifelong learning. It's allowing your brain both stimulation and rest for critical thinking, curiosity, and creativity.

### Signs of Intellectual Wellness[26]

- Development of good study skills and time management
- Ability to challenge yourself to see all sides of an issue
- Becoming a critical thinker
- Development of your ideas, views, and opinions
- Exposing yourself to new ideas, people, and beliefs that are different from your own
- Becoming aware of who you are and what you value

Tiffany's experience working with dental teams reflects the need to open the door to helping team members feel comfortable talking about their goals. Many people don't feel comfortable going to their bosses and talking about their goals. However, nurturing intellectual and professional growth leads to a positive, balanced, and thriving environment for the team and the company.

Quarterly check-ins are a crucial element of our integration process with companies. These conversations allow Tiffany's practice managers or doctors to connect with each employee. It's important to note that this is not a review. Instead, the focus is on discussing where the employee has been, where they are now, and where they are going. It's about setting priorities for the next ninety days.

One topic we emphasize during these conversations is understanding what excites each team member. We ask questions like, "What do you want to learn? Where do you want to grow? How can we support you in that process?" For example, she recalls a front desk employee excited about taking on the responsibility for referral management. The practice introduced a new software program that she needed to learn to excel in this role, providing a mentally stimulating opportunity for growth.

We also stress the importance of core values. If a practice or company values lifelong learning, quarterly conversations can reinforce that principle. By attracting people who share these values, intellectual well-being becomes an integral part of the company culture. This approach helps keep employees mentally engaged and fosters continuous growth through various stimulating activities.

In addition to quarterly check-ins, we advocate conducting quarterly "reflection and roadmap" meetings, encouraging open and transparent communication. The benefits of team-building activities provide further mental stimulation and growth opportunities.

For us, it's all about fostering meaningful conversations that promote intellectual well-being. She seeks to understand what drives each person, where their passions lie, and how the company can nurture their growth. Marni offers assessments for those uncertain about their direction to help them discover their strengths. This process is essential for fostering personal and professional development within the organization.

## Intellectual Wellness: Practical Application

A great idea that practices or corporations can implement to boost intellectual wellness is **creating a book club**. In this structure, everyone in the practice focuses on reading a book. Instead of taking time out of the workday, they could set up a WhatsApp group to keep discussions going without affecting productivity. This platform allows for a structured way of exchanging ideas, asking questions, and expanding perspectives, experiences, and knowledge.

For example, one company Tiffany worked with started reading *Unreasonable Hospitality* by Will Guidara. The team adopted a new approach to hospitality, learning collectively and growing together.

Another way teams can engage intellectually and bond is by participating in events outside the office, such as races or walks for a cause, like the Race for the Cure or an Alzheimer's walk. These activities deliver intellectual stimulation and team bonding by achieving something together outside their daily routines. Achievement fosters personal and professional growth and creates a sense of accomplishment and pride.

We encourage leaders to give teams opportunities for self-discovery. Rather than just providing answers, leaders should ask questions like, "What would you do in this situation, and why?" These conversations spark cognitive growth, encourage deeper reasoning and intellectual development, and empower teams to solve problems creatively and critically.

## Social Wellness

Staci, a woman in her late forties, had been a practice manager at a well-regarded periodontal practice for a few years. She was skilled at her job and got along with her team. Despite this, something was missing. Though she worked with a close-knit team, she often felt disconnected. The fast pace of the practice left little time for meaningful interactions, and the team's communication sometimes felt transactional—focused purely on patient care and logistics.

The practice brought our team in to address social wellness. Staci was intrigued and worked closely with us, the doctors, and the entire team to improve social wellness and implement changes throughout the practice.

We encouraged Staci and the team to focus on building authentic connections with one another and patients. One simple change was introducing "check-in" meetings at the start of each week's huddle, where team members could share personal and professional success stories from the last week. Staci led these quick huddles, creating a space where the team could bond over shared experiences, celebrate life milestones, and offer support during tough times.

We also emphasized the importance of effective communication and active listening. With our guidance, Staci became intentional in her interactions— listening more deeply, asking open-ended questions, and engaging in genuine conversation. This shift helped her build stronger relationships with her coworkers, who began to feel more seen and appreciated.

We didn't stop there. We helped Staci create quarterly team-building activities as part of the Reflect and Roadmap. At first, some coworkers were hesitant, but soon, these gatherings became a cherished part of their routine. The activities, whether sharing a meal, playing games, or just laughing together, brought the team closer.

As social wellness flourished, Staci and the doctors noticed profound changes in the practice. The atmosphere became more supportive and collaborative. Communication improved dramatically as team members grew more comfortable voicing their ideas and concerns. The enhanced connection between the staff also created a ripple effect with patients. They sensed the positive energy and warmth from the team, which made their dental visits more enjoyable and made them feel more cared for.

For Staci, the benefits of social wellness extended beyond the workplace. She felt more fulfilled, less stressed, and more excited to come to work each day. The practice became a place where she could thrive professionally and where genuine relationships could flourish. Social wellness transformed the culture, turning what was once a high-functioning team into a truly cohesive, connected community.

**PROTIP**: Active Listening Exercise: Group your team in twos. The facilitator uses a sixty-second timer and sets the rules. Each person has sixty seconds to share something positive that has happened to them recently. The kicker? The listener can't say anything. The listener can use body language and facial expressions only for sixty seconds. Then, after sixty seconds, switch. Take ten minutes afterward to ask for feedback on how the exercise worked for people. Explain that active listening requires being fully present in the conversation. Being present involves listening with all your senses (sight, sound, etc.) and giving your full attention to the speaker.

## As Goes the Leadership Team Goes the Rest of the Company

As we have been discussing, social wellness in the workplace refers to how employees interact with each other, form connections, and maintain meaningful relationships. Social wellness is the fabric of a workplace. Strong social wellness is crucial in creating a positive, thriving environment, while poor social dynamics can breed toxicity.

When leaders focus solely on key performance indicators like sales and overlook the value of social wellness, they are missing a crucial element. Without attention to these interpersonal dynamics, the company will never fully unlock its potential. Leadership is critical in shaping the culture and establishing social wellness standards. "As goes the leadership team, so goes the rest of the organization."

The tone and health of social relationships within a practice or company come from the top. When leaders tolerate or engage in toxic behavior, negativity can spread throughout the office like a cancer. When working with companies, the first two months typically involve establishing core values and clarifying the mission and vision. Once there is a foundation, it becomes clear who will level up with the new direction and who may need to level out. It's a hard reality, especially when those people may have been on the team for a long time. Having the right people in the right seats is essential.

So yes, some people may have to go and find something else to do.

**PROTIP**: personality assessments are an excellent tool for fostering healthy team dynamics.

Personality tests like Myers-Briggs and DISC help leaders and employees better understand themselves and their team members. The insights can also improve communication and collaboration. When people understand their strengths and challenges, as well as those of their colleagues, it creates empathy and allows for a more supportive work environment. It can lead to critical moments of self-discovery and shift perspectives to enhance relationships.

# Myers-Brigg Type Indicator

|  | Introvert | Introvert | Extrovert | Extrovert |  |
|---|---|---|---|---|---|
| Thinking | ISTJ<br>The Inspector | INTJ<br>The Mastermind | ESTJ<br>The Supervisor | ENTJ<br>The Commander | Judging |
| Thinking | ISTP<br>The Craftsman | INTP<br>The Thinker | ESTP<br>The Doer | ENTP<br>The Visionary | Perceiving |
| Feeling | ISFJ<br>The Nurturer | INFJ<br>The Counsellor | ESFJ<br>The Provider | ENFJ<br>The Giver | Judging |
| Feeling | ISFP<br>The Composer | INFP<br>The Idealist | ESFP<br>The Performer | ENFP<br>The Champion | Perceiving |
|  | Sensing | Intuitive | Sensing | Intuitive |  |

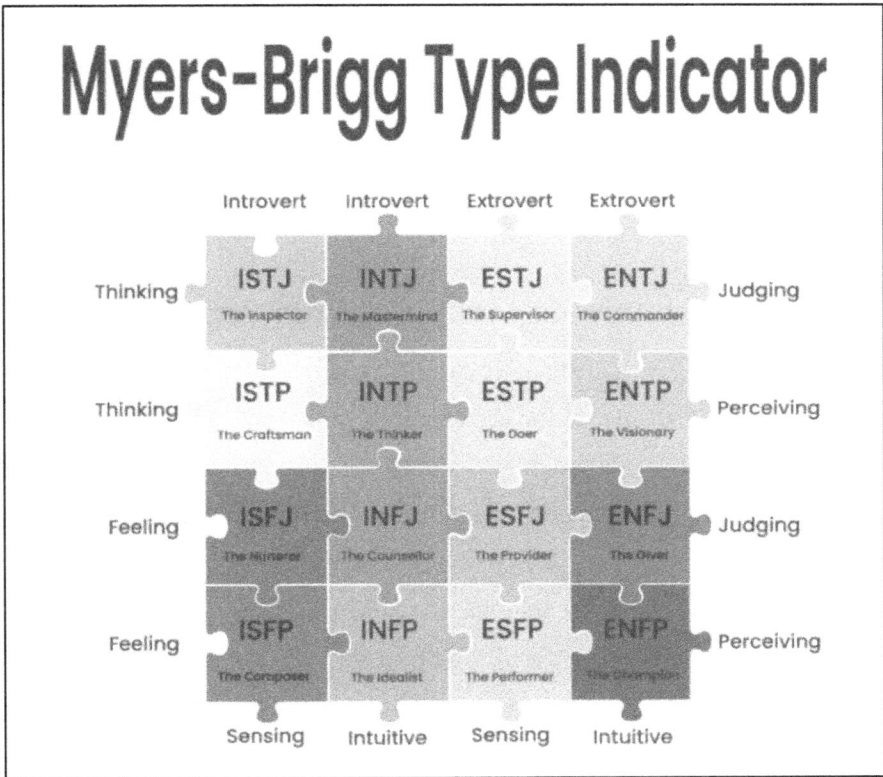

Doing these assessments as a team fosters a deeper sense of connection. Discussing results leads to richer conversations about leveraging those insights for personal and team growth. It's not just about the test results; it's about the collective growth and understanding that emerge from the exercise.

One of the biggest challenges we've all faced post-pandemic is the "Great Resignation." Employee retention relates to how engaged and connected team members feel. If someone doesn't feel a sense of belonging or comfort in the workplace, they are much less likely to stay. Social wellness plays a huge role.

Companies that prioritize relationships keep people engaged. Team bonding experiences, company lunches, and other activities build relationships outside work tasks. Social wellness is also vital from a mental health perspective. The good news is that since the pandemic, the stigma around mental health has greatly diminished.

## Process Documentation is One of Your Keys to Success

The fear of losing long-term staff can be paralyzing for an owner. This is where process documentation comes in. By clearly defining roles and responsibilities and documenting workflow and systems on paper, we reduce the risk associated with transitions. The company can more easily move forward when necessary changes arise, ensuring that lingering toxic behaviors or a lack of clarity do not compromise social wellness. "Be specific or be surprised." Managing transitions with clear, open communication and transparency is critical. Change management creates the foundation for lasting social health in any organization.

### How to Begin Process Documentation?

**Clarify**

- HR, Marketing, Sales, Operations (how you deliver your product or service), Finance, and Customer Support
- Identify a few of the CORE processes (the 20% that creates 80% of the results)

**Record**

- Use a Google Drive MS Word document
- Record the major steps in each of your processes

- Each large step can be supported by the sub-bullets defining the process
- Keep it simple

**Update**

- Review these processes annually to make updates

\* \* \* \*

Tiffany is grateful to work with some great teams. She has a large dental practice that she works with that has over twenty team members, most of whom have been with the business for twenty-plus years. This is a testament to the strong, positive culture of the organization. This impressive retention rate comes from team bonding activities that reflect the business's commitment to inclusivity and community.

Team bonding activities enhance team cohesion and morale. These activities allow team members to connect, share a meal, build rapport, and strengthen interpersonal relationships. Whether it's the adrenaline rush of hitting a bullseye at an axe-throwing competition or the shared sense of achievement after completing a charity walk, these experiences foster a sense of unity and belonging.

Such activities are strategic investments in the team's overall job satisfaction and engagement. Participating in inclusive events makes team members feel valued and appreciated, boosting their dedication to the practice and each other. These also serve as a platform for team members to showcase different skills and talents, contributing to a richer, more dynamic workplace culture.

These bonding activities reflect the practice's commitment to an environment where collaboration and support are paramount. They encourage open communication and break down hierarchical barriers, allowing team members to interact freely and share ideas. The positive energy from these outings carries over into the workplace, improving team dynamics and productivity.

The benefits extend beyond the team. They positively impact client interactions. Clients can sense the camaraderie and enthusiasm, leading to superior service experiences and contributing to the business's long-term success.

Prioritizing team bonding reinforces an inclusive and supportive culture and ensures members are motivated, engaged, and aligned with the organization's goals. This holistic approach to team building is a key driver of success. A cohesive and inclusive workplace profoundly impacts team members and the business. Being with individuals who foster our professional and personal growth is important. Engaging socially with colleagues boosts confidence and strengthens relationships, ultimately enhancing overall development and job satisfaction.

Fact: Humans need social support from family, friends, or coworkers. Social support can take many forms: emotional, instrumental, and informational:

- **Emotional support** involves empathy and understanding, being there for someone when they are stressed or struggling.
- **Instrumental support** might include tangible help, like providing resources or assistance during a difficult time.
- **Informational support** involves sharing knowledge, like reminding someone about an employee assistance program.

The different types of social support are critical for creating a strong sense of community within the workplace.

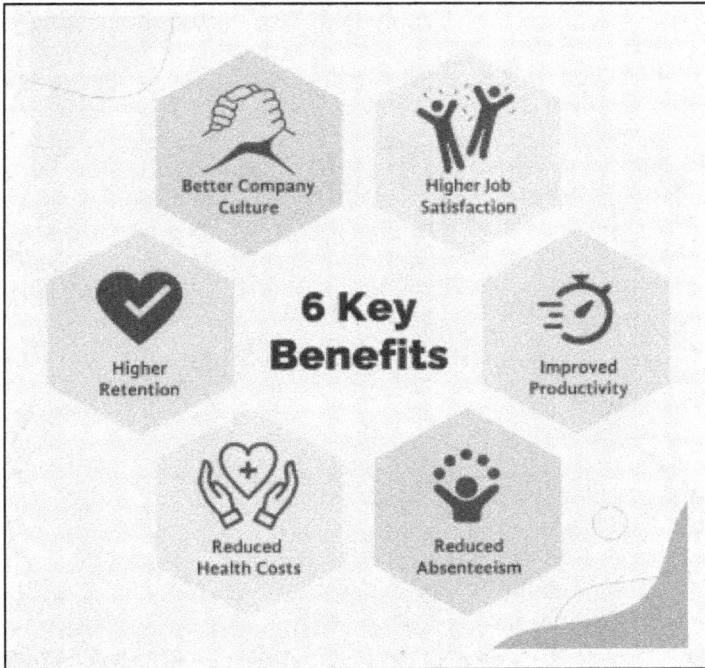

We also emphasize collecting feedback to assess the team's needs. Collecting feedback allows leadership to set measurable goals and create SMARTER (Specific, measurable, Attainable, Results-Oriented, Trackable, Ethical, Rewarding) plans with clear timelines and budgets for improvement. Seeking feedback ensures continuous improvement in social wellness.

Recognition programs are a great example of fostering social wellness. When employees feel valued by their peers, this significantly strengthens social bonds.

In companies we work with, we implement "brag boards or shout-out boards"—simple whiteboards in break rooms where team members can leave notes recognizing each other's accomplishments. It's incredible how this creates a ripple effect of positivity. In one company, a team member even started adding jokes and riddles to the board, making it a fun and engaging way to connect. It becomes self-sustaining, reinforcing a culture of appreciation.

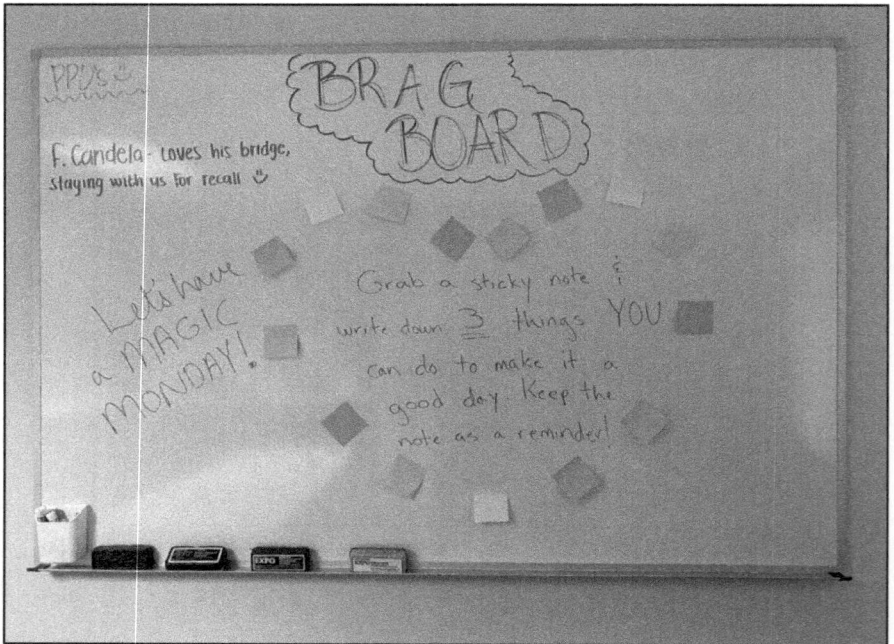

Gallup research [27]shows that employees who lack meaningful connections are nine times more likely to feel disengaged and three times more likely to look for a new job. Strong relationships at work build emotional resilience, helping employees manage stress and set healthy boundaries. The financial impact is staggering, with an estimated $322 billion lost globally due to employee burnout. Creating a culture of recognition and connection supports employees' wellness and improves the business's bottom line.

Social well-being is an essential component of a thriving company. We've seen time and again that companies with strong, positive cultures attract and retain top talent, and social media plays a huge role in this. In today's world, businesses showcase their culture online—highlighting team accomplishments, offering gratitude, and posting fun, organic moments of connection. This fosters a sense of pride within the team and attracts potential new hires drawn to the positive energy and camaraderie.

## To Dance or Not to Dance

Doing fun things like doing dancing videos on social media isn't a good fit for every company and brand, and that's okay. What's most critical is recognizing the value of social wellness and finding ways to showcase your culture. Some teams may highlight their fun and playful sides. Others may express their appreciation and gratitude more professionally. It's all about what resonates with your particular business.

Every organization should find ways to highlight its positive work environment, show appreciation for its team, and share its culture, whether through social media or internal initiatives. Whether it's fun, lighthearted videos, or more traditional recognitions, the goal is to project a strong, healthy, and supportive culture. That's where the magic happens in terms of retention and employee satisfaction.

What matters is that the recognition is there; it's directly tied to social wellness. As we've discussed, social wellness greatly affects how engaged, connected, and ultimately happy employees feel in their workplace. So whether you're a more reserved company or one that leans into a fun-loving, high-energy vibe, you can find your unique way to elevate your team and communicate that sense of appreciation and belonging.

**Culture is everything**. It's the foundation on which successful teams and thriving businesses are built. When prioritizing social wellness, we create environments where people feel valued, connected, and inspired to do their best work. Systems, operations, and financial growth naturally follow when we first focus on cultivating a healthy, supportive culture.

# Environmental Wellness

Karen, a physical therapist in her fifties, had been running her small, successful physical therapy practice for over twenty years. Her clinic was a go-to for personalized care and rehabilitation. Karen had been thinking about how to evolve her business. While she was great at helping her patients heal physically, she found an aspect of well-being she hadn't considered: environmental wellness.

A local sustainability workshop inspired Karen to integrate environmental wellness into her clinic. She learned that our physical spaces impact our health and well-being and that creating a more eco-friendly, natural environment could benefit both her patients and staff.

Karen started small. She replaced the harsh fluorescent lights in her clinic with energy-efficient lighting that mimicked natural sunlight to create a relaxing, healing atmosphere. Next, she introduced plants, knowing greenery could improve air quality and reduce stress. Patients immediately noticed the shift.

Karen looked for other ways to incorporate environmental wellness into her practice. She switched to eco-friendly cleaning products to avoid harsh chemicals that could irritate patients, especially those with respiratory issues. She also started using sustainable materials for therapy tools, like wooden massage rollers and organic, hypoallergenic lotions.

Karen's next step was more ambitious. She installed motion-sensor lights in less frequently used areas and upgraded the heating and cooling systems to be more energy efficient. She also invested in reusable, washable therapy bands and towels, reducing waste.

The benefits were immediate and far-reaching. Patients raved about how the clinic felt more peaceful and welcoming. Many commented that they felt more relaxed during their therapy sessions. The soothing environment sped recovery times for some, as they felt more motivated to engage in their treatments.

Her staff noticed the difference. The cleaner air, natural light, and positive atmosphere improved morale and energy levels. Team members took fewer sick days and increased productivity. Employees were proud to be part of a clinic prioritizing the planet and their well-being.

Karen was initially cautious about the investments, but within a year, she saw the returns. Energy costs dropped, and patient referrals grew. High-quality care and commitment to environmental wellness were the keys. The business's reputation grew as a sustainable and holistic place of healing, attracting clients who shared those values.

Embracing environmental wellness improved Karen's business and transformed her sense of purpose. By aligning her practice with sustainability and creating a healing environment, Karen helped patients recover physically and contributed to their overall well-being and the planet's health. Her small clinic became a shining example of how even healthcare businesses could embrace eco-friendly principles to benefit everyone involved.

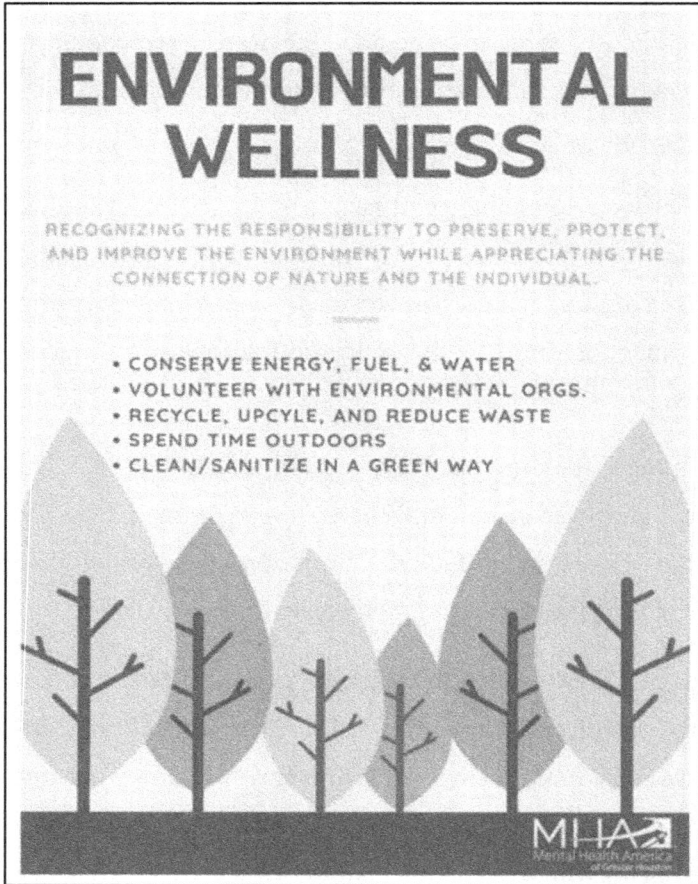

## Supporting Well-Being in Your Business

Working in a pleasant, stimulating environment supports well-being and improves environmental wellness. It promotes interaction with nature and creates an enjoyable personal environment (both in and out of your workspace).

## Signs of Environmental Wellness[28]

- Being aware of the limits of the earth's natural resources
- Conserving energy (i.e., shutting off unused lights)
- Recycling paper, cans, and glass as much as possible
- Enjoying and appreciating time outside in natural settings
- Not polluting the air, water, or earth
- Creating home and work environments that are supportive and nurturing

Environmental wellness is crucial in overall well-being, productivity, and job satisfaction, especially within an office or practice. Though often overlooked, the physical environment where employees spend most of their time can significantly impact how they feel, think, and work.

When we consider environmental wellness in the workplace, it comes down to a few key elements: comfort, ergonomics, and environment. These factors can enhance the workplace experience and improve performance and employee satisfaction.

## Office Ergonomics: More than Just a Better Chair

Ergonomics is the core of environmental wellness. It focuses on designing workspaces to minimize discomfort and maximize efficiency. Ergonomics includes everything from the chairs employees sit on to how they interact with their phones, computers, and even the layout of their workstations. Something as simple as a poorly designed chair can lead to long-term health issues, particularly for employees who spend most of their day sitting.

Dental hygienists often struggle with shoulder and neck pain due to the awkward positions they must maintain at work. For Tiffany, who spent twenty years as a dental hygienist, getting a more ergonomic chair was a game-changer. This simple adjustment improved her comfort and performance. Her proactive step highlights an essential point: leadership should ensure employees are comfortable in their working environment before discomfort becomes an issue. If employees have to ask for ergonomic solutions, it's often too late—they're already in pain.

That's why employers must ask their staff, "Are you comfortable? What do you need to perform your duties in a way that feels good?" By addressing these questions before issues arise, employers not only prevent discomfort but also demonstrate care for their employees' well-being. Employees who feel physically well will be more engaged, focused, and capable of doing their best work.

## The Proactive Approach: Surveys and Regular Check-Ins

Conducting regular surveys or check-ins with employees helps ensure ongoing comfort and satisfaction in the workplace. A proactive approach to workplace wellness can be as simple as sending a survey twice a year, asking employees what changes or improvements could make their environment more comfortable. This allows leadership to avoid potential issues rather than react to problems after they've caused discomfort or stress.

When employees feel comfortable, they're more engaged with their work, more connected to their team, and more likely to be satisfied overall. There is a ripple effect: **happier employees create more positive interactions with clients or patients, and that energy spreads.** This can be especially impactful in healthcare settings like dental or medical practices, as the quality of care is directly linked to the working environment.

## Small Changes, Big Impact

Beyond ergonomics, small environmental changes can significantly impact employee well-being. For example, introducing healthy snacks in the breakroom, as one of our client companies did, sends a message that the company cares about the health and comfort of its staff. This attention to detail can make a busy and demanding job more manageable, especially during peak times.

Ensuring that equipment functions properly is another essential piece of the puzzle. For example, one way to reduce "silent stressors" is allowing employees to report broken equipment and request repair without management approval. By empowering employees to take immediate action, businesses reduce unnecessary frustration and help their teams maintain a smooth, productive workflow.

## The Importance of Functional Design

When designing or renovating an office space, it's essential to consider function over fashion. While aesthetic appeal matters, designing workspaces that are functional and tailored to specific tasks is more important. For example, placing essential tools or supplies in hard-to-reach locations might look good in a new office design. However, it can lead to repetitive strain injuries if employees have to bend or reach awkwardly multiple times a day.

We recall a story of a client with a med spa. She did a beautiful renovation she was proud of. Unfortunately, she didn't ask the massage therapists for their input and placed towels in lower cabinets, which created strain on the therapists.

Involving ergonomics experts early in the design process can help avoid these mistakes. Someone like Caitlin Parsons (www.TheAlignedHygienist.com), who specializes in ergonomics, can evaluate a workspace and identify areas for improvement, ensuring that the environment supports employees' long-term health and productivity.

Ergonomics creates a workspace that reduces strain, supports health, and allows your team to work comfortably and efficiently. Across industries, repetitive movements, static postures, and awkward positioning can lead to fatigue, discomfort, and injury. An ergonomically designed workspace promotes well-being, productivity, and career longevity.

A well-designed workspace is essential. Position frequently used tools, equipment, and supplies within easy reach to minimize twisting, bending, and overreaching. Adjustable desks and chairs that support neutral posture reduce strain on the back, neck, and shoulders. Monitors should be placed at eye level, and task lighting should be positioned to reduce glare and minimize eye strain. For roles requiring specialized equipment, ensure tools are easily accessible and ergonomically aligned to the task.

A proactive approach to ergonomics begins with investing in the right tools. Chairs and workstations should be adjustable and tailored to each individual's needs. Lightweight tools, flexible cords, and equipment that minimize repetitive motions reduce physical strain on employees. Regular maintenance of tools and equipment ensures they operate efficiently and require less force or effort.

Incorporating wellness practices like microbreaks and stretching into daily routines helps your team stay refreshed and energized. Starting meetings with wellness reminders or brief stretches can make these habits part of your company culture. Employers should also prioritize ergonomic training, conduct regular assessments of workspaces, and encourage open communication about comfort and support needs.

By prioritizing ergonomics and wellness, you create a healthier, more engaged team, fostering productivity, job satisfaction, and long-term success for your business.

Hartford's 2023 Future of Benefits Report [29] emphasizes that 78% of employers are interested in employee wellness. Innovative workplace design is an effective way to enhance employee well-being over the long term.

## Natural Light, Air Quality, and Green Spaces

While ergonomics and functionality are critical components of environmental wellness, other factors, like natural light and air quality, also significantly affect how employees feel throughout the workday. Businesses should position workstations to maximize exposure to natural light, which has been shown to improve mood and productivity. Adequate ventilation and air quality are equally important; fresh air helps employees stay alert and focused.

Introducing non-toxic cleaning products and indoor plants contributes to a healthier office environment. Indoor plants improve air quality and provide a sense of calm and connection to nature, reducing stress and enhancing overall well-being.

## Decluttering for a Clear Mind

A cluttered, messy workspace can be a source of stress for employees, making them feel disorganized or overwhelmed. There is a direct connection between a clean, well-organized workspace and how employees feel. The cleanliness and order of the office impact both the employee experience and the impression clients have of the business. It is worth investing in regular cleaning services and encouraging employees to keep their workstations clutter-free. A clean office benefits clients and creates a sense of security and comfort for employees, helping them feel more at ease and focused on their tasks.

Employers demonstrate that they value their employees' well-being by taking proactive steps to enhance the workplace's physical environment. This commitment to environmental wellness improves the daily work experience and contributes to long-term job satisfaction, employee retention, and a positive culture.

A positive culture and great vibe in the workplace significantly boost retention by fostering a sense of belonging and satisfaction among employees. Environmental wellness and a thriving workplace culture are pivotal in enhancing the overall success of a business. When companies prioritize a healthy and supportive environment, they boost employee morale and a sense of belonging and commitment. This can increase innovation and creativity, as employees feel comfortable and encouraged to share their ideas. These efforts demonstrate a commitment to employee well-being and environmental responsibility, aligning with a broader cultural shift toward sustainability.

Google is a shining example of how a positive work environment can enhance team happiness, productivity, and retention. Known for its vibrant office spaces, Google offers a range of perks that cater to the diverse needs of its employees. From on-site fitness centers and nap pods to gourmet meals and flexible work arrangements, Google prioritizes employee satisfaction and work-life balance. This commitment to a supportive culture attracts top talent and ensures employees remain engaged and motivated.

Google has maintained its reputation as a leader in innovation and employee satisfaction, fostering an environment where creativity and collaboration are encouraged.

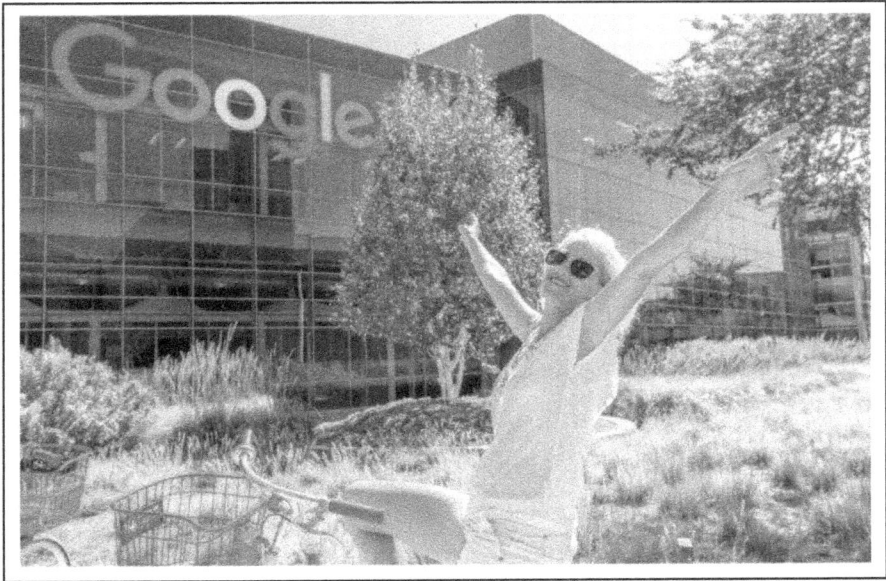

The impact of environmental wellness and a positive culture extends beyond individual companies, influencing industry standards and expectations. When businesses invest in their employees' well-being and create an inclusive, sustainable workplace, they cultivate loyalty and reduce turnover. This leads to cost savings in recruitment and training and strengthens team cohesion and productivity. By prioritizing environmental wellness and positive culture, businesses can achieve sustainable success and create a lasting impact on their employees' lives and the broader community.

# Financial Wellness

Financial wellness is the ability to meet basic needs and manage money for the short- and long-term. In Tiffany's first book, *"Hygienepreneur: The Dental Hygienist's Guide to Achieving Career Success and Personal Transformation,"* she dedicated a chapter to finding financial tranquility. This topic held deep significance for her, having lived with financial stress for much of her life. She finally attained meaningful financial stability when she built her practice and business. Her employer's support was crucial, as it wasn't solely about the salary; it was about nurturing her intellectual growth and deepening her understanding of finances.

A personal experience inspired a chapter in her book. Her boss gifted copies of Dave Ramsey's *Financial Peace* book and workbook to each team member one Christmas. Although he didn't know the specifics of their financial situations, he consciously tried to empower the team with knowledge. He already supported them with fair wages, solid benefits, and performance bonuses, but this gesture was different. It was about equipping them with tools to manage their finances. His support for their financial literacy had a transformative effect. It elevated the culture of the practice and boosted employee satisfaction.

As Tiffany and her colleagues dove into Ramsey's teachings, they began collaborating and sharing insights. They held regular meetings to discuss their insights. This simple Christmas gift evolved into a shared mission of personal financial growth. It gave them the impetus to reflect on their financial goals.

Supporting employees is a crucial strategy for businesses. It doesn't require a massive overhaul; it can be as simple as providing access to financial literacy resources or sending employees to workshops on retirement planning. An alarming number of employees aren't equipped to manage their retirement funds; even a basic course can make a tremendous difference.

In Tiffany's book, she offers various resources for financial security. While she doesn't claim to be a financial expert, her experiences have given her invaluable insights. Finding what resonates with you makes you feel in control of your financial wellness. She advocates financial literacy programs within companies to reduce stress and empower employees. Statistics show that 76% of employees say financial stress affects their productivity, and 55% lose at least three hours of work each week worrying about finances.[30]

Businesses can ease this burden by offering financial wellness programs. Start with a survey to understand what employees need—help with retirement planning, paying off student debt, or saving for a home. Starting early with financial literacy has long-lasting benefits. While many employees might not seek out these opportunities independently, they are more likely to engage when leadership provides them.

Receiving financial peace as a Christmas gift was transformative. It showed that my boss cared enough to provide me with valuable knowledge unrelated to work. Many colleagues shared that they had never received financial guidance from their parents, making the information all the more crucial. Regardless of size, any company can provide financial literacy training, enhancing individual employees and overall business success.

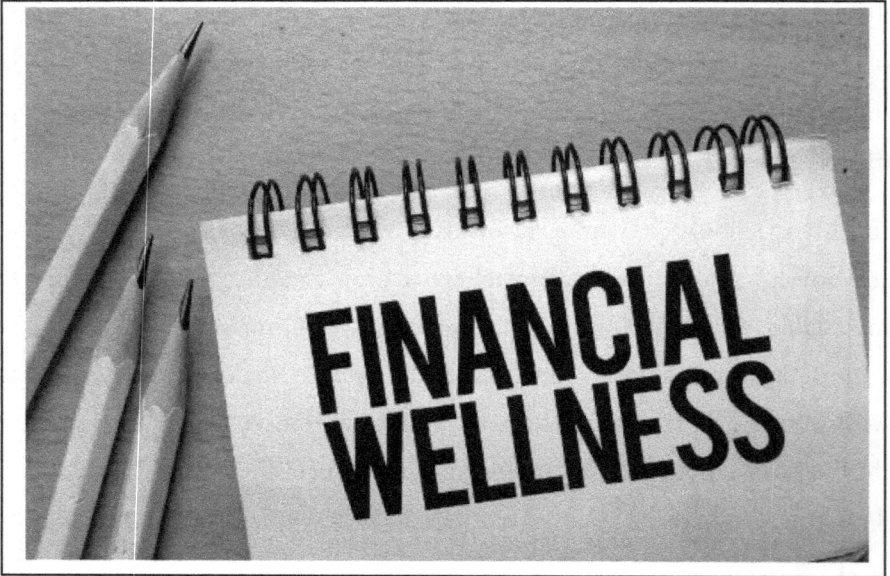

## Signs of Financial Wellness [31]

- Learning how to manage your money and establishing a personal budget

- Not living beyond your means

- Making a plan to pay back your student loans

- Learning about debt and how to manage it

- Building good credit

- Thinking long term, e.g., setting up a savings account, setting up investments, and a retirement account

- Learning not to let money be the driving force of your life or an indication of your self-worth

- Donating some of your money, if possible, to a cause you believe in

Many employees live paycheck to paycheck and worry about retirement. When employers integrate financial wellness into their benefits package, they provide a pathway to alleviate this stress, directly impacting productivity. Financial worries consume significant mental energy; businesses should address the issue head-on.

The first step is open communication. Businesses must understand the team's financial needs. Tailoring financial wellness programs to employees is key. Providing resources from experts gives team members access to practical tools and knowledge.

The sooner employees invest in their financial future, the better their long-term outcomes. Incentives to participate in financial programs and employee access at all stages ensure inclusivity. Younger employees might need help budgeting, while older employees may focus on retirement planning.

We've seen how powerful it is when leadership teams show they care about their employees' financial well-being. It's not just about numbers—it's about improving morale, productivity, and loyalty.

# SECTION II
## EMOTIONAL INTELLIGENCE

# EMOTIONAL INTELLIGENCE

## Tiffany's Story

I remember going to my first Brendon Burchard Event. I showed up on January 1st, ready to start my year off right. I had a goal to learn something new that day. I experienced an energy that sparked personal and professional growth.

I felt it the minute I arrived. The attendees were buzzing with excitement. They were all there seeking the same spark. The same transformation led them to the "answer" that we were all looking for. I was a high achiever who was not satisfied. I suspected many in the room were just like me. We were professionals who wanted to achieve more and experience "next-level" greatness in our careers and relationships.

When Brendon came on stage, the music and the vibe were positive and energizing. It was the perfect start to a great day of learning through self-discovery. That day, he spoke about emotional regulation. This piece of the puzzle would lead me toward more peace and understanding.

Brendon cupped his hand over his heart like a dial. He demonstrated the act of dialing an emotion up or down. This visualization of controlling my emotions blew my mind. This physical gesture is a grounding tool, helping individuals tune into their emotional state and regain control. Brendon Burchard's self-regulation technique emphasizes **intentional living**. Through mindful practices, individuals learn to navigate challenges more effectively, leading to personal and professional growth.

I experienced this at the event. I had the power to control my thoughts, and this strategy would drive my positive experiences from that point forward.

## Marni's Story

Honestly, I didn't even understand emotions until I was around thirty years old. I grew up in a family where emotions were often swept under the rug. It wasn't considered appropriate to express emotions. As I grew into adulthood, I was unequipped to deal with emotion.

Many of us have grown up in similar environments. We were never taught how to navigate our emotions, and as adults, everyone assumes we know how to regulate ourselves in every situation.

Emotional regulation is a learned skill. Constantly stuffing emotions down is that, much like sweeping things under the rug, eventually, you're going to trip and hurt yourself. That's a direct analogy to what happens when we don't address our emotions. If we don't learn how to manage them, they control us.

It's taken me thirty years to build this skill set, so I know it's possible to learn. As a young person, I didn't know how to articulate what I was feeling—I just knew I felt bad, and I'd cry. Now, I talk to my teams about how emotions can physically manifest in the body. It's like a warning light on a car's dashboard—an indicator that something is off internally. When you start to feel a shortness of breath, a tightness in your chest, or your face getting hot, your body is alerting you to an emotional response.

Well-known dog trainer Cesar Millan refers to a "red zone" dogs go into. When we start to feel those physical signs, it's a signal that we're headed into an emotional red zone. If we recognize those signs, we can take control before those emotions take over. When emotions control us, we risk damaging our credibility and relationships.

## What is Emotional Intelligence?

Emotional intelligence refers to the ability to understand and regulate your own emotions while also recognizing and influencing the emotions of others. Originally introduced in 1990 by researchers John Mayer and Peter Salovey, the concept gained wider recognition through the work of psychologist Daniel Goleman.

Over a decade ago, Goleman emphasized the significance of emotional intelligence in leadership, stating in the Harvard Business Review, *"The most effective leaders share one essential trait: a high level of emotional intelligence. While IQ and technical skills are important, they are merely baseline qualifications for executive roles."*[32]

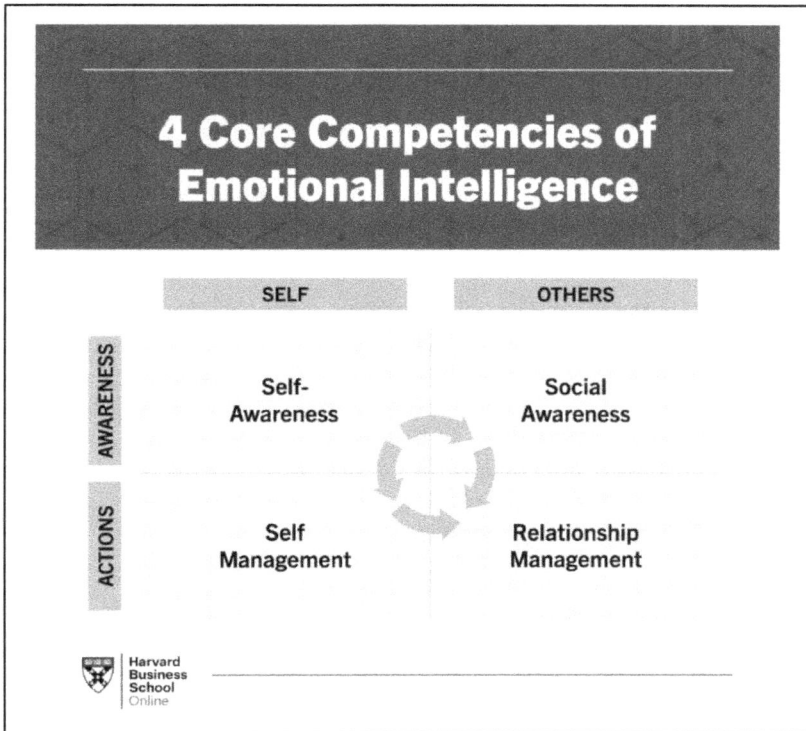

**4 Core Competencies of Emotional Intelligence**

|  | SELF | OTHERS |
|---|---|---|
| **AWARENESS** | Self-Awareness | Social Awareness |
| **ACTIONS** | Self Management | Relationship Management |

Harvard Business School Online

# Recognizing a Lack of Emotional Intelligence

Poor emotional intelligence often leads to workplace conflicts and misunderstandings. These issues stem from the inability to recognize or understand emotions. Difficulty managing and expressing emotions is a key sign of low emotional intelligence. This difficulty may appear as struggles in addressing colleagues' concerns or active listening.

Evaluate your workplace relationships by asking yourself:

- Are conversations with colleagues tense?
- Do you often blame others when things go wrong?
- Are you prone to emotional outbursts?

These behaviors indicate a lack of emotional intelligence. Social skills and empathy are the core elements of emotional intelligence. If you want to improve, these are the issues to address.

# The Four Components of Emotional Intelligence

Emotional intelligence consists of four main competencies:

- Self-awareness
- Self-management
- Social awareness
- Relationship management

Each of these components plays a crucial role in developing emotional intelligence. Here's a closer look at each one:

## 1. Self-Awareness

Self-awareness is the foundation of emotional intelligence. It involves recognizing your strengths, weaknesses, and emotions and understanding how they affect your performance and team.

Research by organizational psychologist Tasha Eurich shows that while 95% of people believe they are self-aware, only 10-15% truly are. [33] This lack of self-awareness can impact team success, increase stress, and reduce motivation.

## 2. Self-Management

Self-management involves controlling your emotions, especially in stressful situations, and maintaining a positive attitude during challenges. Leaders lacking in self-management may react impulsively and struggle to control their emotions.

Emotional intelligence helps shift responses from reactive to intentional. Practicing self-management might involve taking a breath break or stepping away from a stressful situation to collect your thoughts.

## 3. Social Awareness

In addition to managing your emotions, social awareness involves understanding the emotions and dynamics of those around you. Leaders with strong social awareness practice empathy, helping them communicate and collaborate more effectively.

Empathy has been ranked as the top leadership skill. Leaders who excel in this area perform better in coaching, engaging others, and decision-making. Showing empathy can significantly enhance team morale and individual performance.

## 4. Relationship Management

Relationship management focuses on your ability to influence, coach, and resolve conflicts effectively. Addressing issues promptly can save time and improve workplace dynamics.

Research shows unresolved conflicts waste company resources and harm morale.[34] Leaders who are skilled at conflict resolution foster better team environments where the respectful treatment of employees is prioritized.

# Strengthening Your Emotional Intelligence

Building emotional intelligence, particularly self-awareness, can be achieved through several methods:

- **Journaling:** Reflect daily on how your emotions affected your decisions and interactions, identifying patterns you want to replicate or avoid.
- **360-Degree Feedback:** Seek feedback from colleagues and compare it to self-assessments to uncover blind spots.
- **Active Listening:** Set distractions aside and fully engage with others by paraphrasing and using non-verbal cues.
- **Emotional Reflection:** When you experience a strong emotion, explore its root cause and how it affects your behavior.
- **Online Training:** Consider courses that offer insights into emotional intelligence, such as leadership programs that include 360-degree assessments.

## The Impact of Emotional Intelligence on Leadership

Leaders set the tone for their organizations. Poor emotional intelligence can result in disengaged employees and higher turnover. Even if you excel in technical skills, your ability to communicate and collaborate with your team is essential for success.

By strengthening emotional intelligence, leaders can foster a more positive work environment, improve interpersonal relationships, and advance their careers and their organizations.

Let's look into the four main components of building emotional intelligence: Emotional regulation, motivation, empathy, compassion, and social skills.

Emotional regulation is deeply rooted in our early beliefs. By age seven, our beliefs already shape how we engage with others. We must challenge these underlying beliefs. When Marni teaches about the growth mindset, she talks about it in relation to emotional regulation. Our beliefs are like computer software. They continue to run in the background unless we eject them and insert new perspectives.

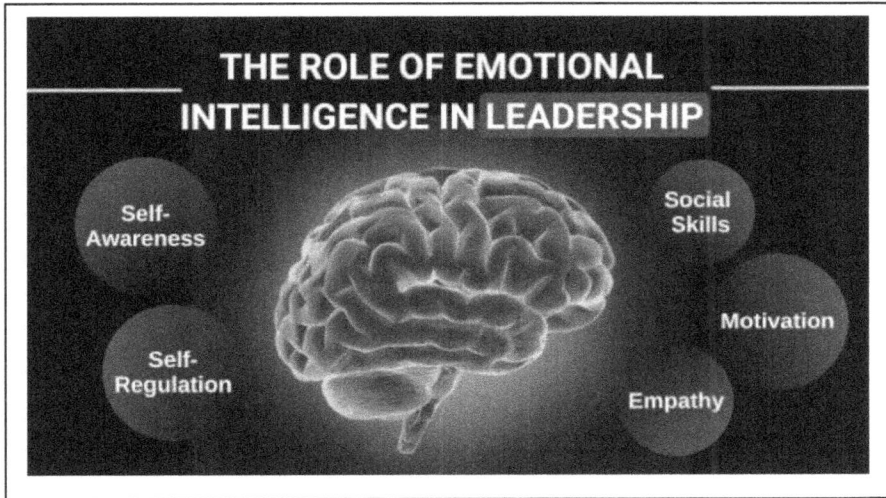

THE ROLE OF EMOTIONAL INTELLIGENCE IN LEADERSHIP

Self-Awareness

Social Skills

Motivation

Self-Regulation

Empathy

Marni's been working with a treatment coordinator in a practice she supported. She's really good at reading other people's body language and selling treatments—best in class—but she struggles with emotional regulation. This makes interpersonal communication with her team difficult. Marni spent months working with her on these skills.

Marni helped her understand that emotions are a normal part of life; some of us experience them in more intense, volatile ways. Emotions are like waves—the highs and lows can overwhelm us if we don't learn to navigate them. Those emotional waves will just keep crashing over us, causing personal damage and hurting our professional credibility.

This is all part of a larger journey to developing emotional intelligence. We'll explore some specific skills you can use to build this emotional regulation. There's a lot to learn, but the payoff is huge—personally and professionally.

*"Emotional intelligence is the ability to understand and manage your emotions, as well as recognize and influence the emotions of those around you."*- **Harvard Business School.**

**Our emotions are dynamic—they are "dual-natured forces."** They can either be your best friends or challenging partners. As you journey through your personal and professional life, emotional regulation leads to a life of more positivity and less stress. Managing emotions is challenging but deeply rewarding. Understanding and managing emotions enhances your professional expertise and personal well-being and relationships.

What are the four pathways to developing emotional intelligence in your business? Emotional regulation, motivation, empathy, compassion, and social skills. So let's discuss those...

## The Crucial Skills to Help Your Team Develop

Emotional regulation has become crucial to individual well-being and organizational effectiveness. Defined as an adaptive ability that impacts mental and physical health, quality of life, and functionality, emotional regulation fosters a positive workplace culture.

Recent studies, including research from reputable institutions like the National Library of Medicine and the National Institutes of Health, highlight emotional intensity's profound influence on emotional regulation.[35]

In one notable study, participants maintained diaries to record instances of strong negative emotions, identifying the specific feelings and the regulatory strategies they used. These strategies were acceptance, reappraisal, rumination, distraction, and suppression.

The findings from this study revealed a critical insight: as the intensity of an emotion increases, individuals are more likely to resort to rumination—**a negative strategy characterized by repetitive thinking about distressing events.** [36] This "hamster wheel" of thought creates patterns in the brain, making it harder for individuals to escape the cycle of negative emotions. To break free from rumination, individuals must develop awareness and adopt healthier strategies for emotional regulation.

## The Role of Leadership in Emotional Regulation

Leaders play a pivotal role in shaping emotional climate. It's common for managers to express frustration with team members struggling with emotional regulation. Every workplace will have individuals with varying degrees of emotional regulation skills, and simply hiring someone new does not guarantee a better outcome.

Leaders must commit to their emotional growth and development. By enhancing their own emotional intelligence, leaders set the tone for the entire team. This includes developing skills in conflict resolution and emotional support, which can create a nurturing environment conducive to personal and professional growth.

An anecdote illustrates this point well: a client of ours expressed doubts about retaining a high-performing employee whose interpersonal skills left much to be desired. While tempted to replace her, we reminded him that leadership is responsible for fostering a supportive environment. He needed to be part of the solution! Developing emotional regulation skills requires patience, empathy, and a commitment to nurturing growth.

## Cultivating Emotional Regulation in High-Pressure Environments

In high-performance workplaces, the intensity of interactions can lead to emotional strain. Developing emotional regulation skills among team members is essential for creating a productive and harmonious work environment. Companies prioritizing emotional intelligence foster a culture of collaboration and respect, ultimately enhancing overall productivity.

As professionals navigate their roles, emotional challenges will arise. Leaders must equip themselves and their teams with the tools to address these challenges. Organizations can ensure that employees and patients receive the highest quality of care by cultivating emotional regulation skills and fostering a supportive atmosphere.

Being NoN-Judgemental ?!

Holding the Good
the Bad and the Neutral
Without Preference

## Breaking Down Emotional Regulation

At its core, emotional regulation is about steering your emotional ship. Whether tackling a tricky client situation or dealing with a personal setback, controlling your emotional response makes all the difference. Emotional regulation involves conscious and unconscious processes. Conscious control is like being the captain of your ship—actively deciding which direction to steer and what to dodge. Unconscious control, on the other hand, is the autopilot mode. Your temperament and experience govern your course. Knowing that the unconscious influences our consciousness is a key component of self-regulation.

## Strategies for Effective Emotional Regulation

One proven approach to emotional regulation is **Dialectical Behavior Therapy (DBT)**, [37]which provides essential coping skills for managing emotions. Originating from the work of psychologist Marsha Linehan, DBT was initially designed to help individuals struggling with severe emotional dysregulation, particularly those at risk of self-harm. However, its principles have since been adapted for broader applications, making it a valuable resource for anyone looking to improve their emotional regulation skills.

DBT focuses on two core strategies: changing emotions and accepting them. It encompasses four primary skills that can be instrumental in the workplace:

- **Acting Opposite:** This strategy encourages individuals to engage in behaviors contrary to their initial emotional responses, helping to create a shift in feelings.
- **Checking the Facts:** This involves evaluating the reality of a situation to determine whether emotional reactions are justified.
- **Pleasing:** This emphasizes the importance of self-care and taking actions that foster positive emotions.
- **Focusing on Positive Results:** Encouraging individuals to recognize and celebrate positive outcomes reinforces a positive mindset and builds resilience.

Implementing these strategies can create a more supportive and emotionally intelligent workplace.

## The Two Sides of Emotional Control

Emotion regulation can be as simple as "turning the volume down" on emotions like anger or anxiety. I have experienced client meetings that didn't go as planned. I felt frustrated and defeated at times. I learned to turn that situation into a more positive one through self-regulation. Instead of letting that frustration get the best of me, I would remember a funny story or take a moment to breathe- these are down-regulation strategies.

On the flip side, up-regulation involves cranking up emotions when you need them most. Are you facing a new challenge? A dash of excitement or anxiety might just be the fuel you need. For example, when I went on stage to speak during my early years of presenting, I would feel a little nervous and unsure. To overcome those feelings, I learned to tell myself something different. I often told myself how "excited" I was to be there. The brain does not know the difference between nervous and excited. The key component to this winning routine was finding my ability to "dial up" the emotion when necessary.

## More Key Strategies To Achieve Emotional Regulation

The first skill we need is **creating space**. When you start to feel those physical sensations indicating that an emotion is rising, the first step is to pause and take a deep breath. Remember our reference earlier in the book to Viktor Frankl? Remember the "power of the pause."

How impactful is that? Taking a moment to follow your breath is essential. Think of your breath like an ocean, with waves coming in and out.

The next step is becoming aware of your feelings. Notice the sensations in your body and identify your emotions. Ask yourself: Am I angry? Am I sad? Am I disappointed? Remember that most emotions stem from love or fear. Often, fear underlies feelings of anger, disappointment, or frustration. To get off the hamster wheel of thought, grab a piece of paper and write the question you are asking yourself, then pause and allow the answer to rise. Then, write down what is coming up for you.

Once you've named your emotions, hold them with neutrality. A phrase like "Isn't it interesting that I'm feeling this way?" allows you to examine what beliefs or situations contribute to your feelings. You may be unable to process everything at the moment, especially if you're triggered at work. However, you can always take a breath, jot down your thoughts, handle immediate tasks, and return to your feelings later.

It's important to differentiate between healthy compartmentalization—where you set aside emotions for later processing—and unhealthy compartmentalization, where you simply bury them. Many self-help approaches promote a positive attitude; however, be careful of falling into "toxic positivity," processing your feelings is crucial. Remember, we don't want you to sweep your feelings under the rug.

As we explore mindfulness, we need to practice non-judgment. Ask yourself what's happening and what story you're telling yourself. The best way to recognize that you are telling a story is to see if you can create another story.

When Marni was in her early twenties, she had the opportunity to coach with Joseph Russo in New York City. Joseph was an integral part of helping Marni develop many of the skills and foundation that she uses for emotional regulation. One day, during a group session, Joseph talked about the stories we tell ourselves. Marni remembers trying to get to that class that night, which started promptly at seven pm. It was held in a dance studio on 72$^{nd}$ Street and Columbus Avenue.

At the time, Marni worked downtown on the west side. She had to take the subway, and on the way up the stairs, there was a man running up that almost knocked her over. Initially, Marni was annoyed, and she thought to herself that the man had no manners and must not have been raised right. After her session with Joseph and the group that night, she had a different perspective.

She realized there were many stories she could tell about why that man may have been running up so quickly and it may or may not have had anything to do with how he was raised! He could have had to really go to the restroom, for example, or perhaps there was an emergency. As she considered how many stories she could create, she realized that the mind creates stories to help us make sense of the world. These stories are created automatically, and they are based on our own perceptions and experiences. If you can tell a different story about a situation, then you know it's a story you just created.

Consider how you can shift your perspective and choose how to respond. These strategies are vital for navigating emotions and coasting through challenging situations.

I recall a recent conversation with a client team member who felt bullied at work. She insisted we implement an anti-bullying policy. She didn't realize how her behavior contributed to the negative interactions. Our emotional regulation influences how others respond to us, creating a dynamic interaction. Ultimately, effective emotional regulation allows us to coexist peacefully with others.

## Do You Keep The Non-Regulated Employee or Let Them Go?

Let me share a funny story about a practice manager we worked with. We were discussing his team's emotional regulation skills. He focused on one high-performing employee struggling with emotional control. He said, *"I don't know if it's worth keeping her. Maybe we'd be better off starting fresh with someone new."*

He was frustrated, unsure, and unprepared to deal with the situation. I told him, "*Wherever you go, there you are. People are people. You can hire someone who seems perfectly regulated, but everyone faces challenges. As leaders, we must develop the skills to guide our teams through these situations.*"

Leadership isn't about replacing people when things get tough. It's about stepping up, taking responsibility, and growing to lead others through difficult moments. The more self-aware and emotionally regulated you are as a leader, the more you can help your team develop those skills. When emotionally stable, the team can provide the best customer service. If a person can't regulate themselves or communicate well with teammates, how can they be fully present for their patients or clients?

I had to be direct with this manager. I said, "*This is your job. You must develop conflict resolution skills and learn how to support your team in their emotional growth. You must create an environment where people can thrive. You don't need to be a therapist—if someone is dealing with serious issues like depression or suicidal thoughts, that's a different matter. But everyday interpersonal challenges are your responsibility to manage."*

As leaders, we weren't born knowing how to do all this. I wasn't the best leader on day one, but I grew through learning, attending courses, and seeking guidance from others. Business owners must develop leadership skills. They must lead by example, hold people accountable, and address emotions with empathy. When someone on your team lacks a skill, it's your role to nurture and guide them, providing the tools and training they need to grow personally and professionally.

"Let's just get rid of them" is not the solution. No matter who you hire, you'll face similar challenges. Every person is at a different level of emotional regulation. When leaders have the right skills, we foster growth, positivity, and positive change within our teams.

## Bullying - Multiple Perspectives at Play

When someone says, "I'm being bullied," it's important to recognize that multiple perspectives are at play. Each person involved has a role in the dynamic. We all bear responsibility for our actions, reactions, and the outcomes that arise from them.

Dr. Mark Brackett is the founding director of Yale's Center for Emotional Intelligence. His RULER model for emotional self-regulation emphasizes five key components: **Recognizing, Understanding, Labeling, Expressing, and Regulating** emotions. [38] This framework has been beneficial for many of his clients.

**Recognizing** is the first step in identifying emotions in ourselves and others. This is about being open and vulnerable—essentially wearing your heart on your sleeve, which you often advocate for by encouraging authenticity.

**Understanding** involves digging into the triggers that cause our emotions.

**Labeling** is the process of finding the right words to describe our feelings. Labeling our emotions gives us clarity, which can help us manage and downgrade our feelings.

**Expressing** is about identifying our feelings and learning to respond appropriately in social situations. This skill is developed over time.

**Regulating** is learning to suppress our initial reactions, such as anger or frustration. We can respond more effectively by acknowledging our feelings and taking a moment to breathe.

Because emotions are bi-directional, how we respond can elicit different reactions from others. If the response we receive isn't what we hoped for, we may need to step away from the situation. Taking a break can diffuse tension and lead to a better outcome when we revisit the conversation later.

When my team members come to me with issues like feeling unheard or mistreated, we reflect on our actions. For instance, if I text a friend and don't receive a reply, I remind myself that they might just be busy. The same applies in the workplace.

In fast-paced environments, it's common for team members to react quickly, which can come across as brusque or indifferent. When someone feels a colleague was short with them, I encourage them to shift their mindset. Also, we all need to stop taking things so personally. Another one of our favorite books by Don Miquel Ruiz, called The Four Agreements, talks about this very thing.

"Whatever happens around you, don't take it personally... Nothing other people do is because of you. It is because of themselves. All people live in their own dreams, in their own minds; they are in a completely different world from the one we live in. When we take something personally, we make the assumption that they know what is in our world, and we try to impose our world on their world.

Even when a situation seems so personal, even if others insult you directly, it has nothing to do with you. What they say, what they do, and the opinions they give are according to the agreements they have in their own minds...Taking things personally makes you easy prey for these predators, the black magicians. They can hook you easily with one little opinion and feed you whatever poison they want, and because you take it personally, you eat it up. But if you do not take it personally, you are immune in the middle of hell. Immunity in the middle of hell is the gift of this agreement."

Perhaps that person was simply focused on getting the job done. By changing our perspective, we see that there's likely no ill will behind their actions.

Adjusting our thought processes can significantly improve interactions and create a more positive environment for everyone. When we recognize our part in these dynamics, we open the door to better communication and understanding.

## Additional Practical Strategies for Emotional Regulation

1. **Reappraisal:** Change the narrative. See every challenge as an opportunity. When an interaction doesn't go as expected, think of it as a learning moment, not a failure. Define the key takeaways and use them as an opportunity for growth.

2. **Suppression:** Sometimes, keeping a lid on your emotions is necessary. Don't let it become a habit, leading to negative outcomes. It is better to take the pause you need and return to the situation with a different mindset than to bury it. It feels so good when we can use that approach.

3. **Mindful Acceptance**: Acknowledge your emotions without judgment. Let them rise and fall like a wave. Giving ourselves grace is a skill all on its own. Most high-achievers are critical of themselves as they strive for "greatness." It is important to give yourself a "pass."

4. **Attention Shifting**: Focus on something else! Distract yourself from the source of negativity. Listen to a podcast, go for a walk, or have a quick chat with a colleague. Movement boosts mental well-being by reducing stress, anxiety, and depression while enhancing mood and cognitive function. Additionally, promoting a more positive state of mind encourages a constructive approach to problem-solving and uplifts mood. The tool of distraction acts as a natural mood lifter, helping individuals tackle challenges with optimism and creativity.

5. **Reframing:** Turn setbacks into stepping stones. Reframing setbacks as stepping stones transforms perceived failures into growth opportunities. Instead of seeing mistakes as dead ends, view them as valuable lessons that guide your path forward. For instance, if a

project doesn't succeed, analyze what went wrong and apply those insights to future endeavors. Consider the setback as a temporary obstacle to learn from. This perspective builds resilience, enabling you to face challenges positively and be willing to adapt and grow.

## The Importance of Emotional Regulation

Why is emotional regulation crucial? Emotions are the "steering wheel" of your life. You need to hold on! You can gracefully navigate professional and personal storms when you're in control. Poor emotional regulation leads to regretful actions, strained relationships, and missed opportunities.

## Challenges in Emotional Regulation

Controlling emotions isn't always easy. Certain beliefs, like thinking negative emotions are inherently bad, can hinder your progress. Powerful emotions triggered by high-stakes situations can be challenging. But it's a skill that can be honed with practice and patience.

As a leader, I have learned to be patient and give myself grace. We are always growing and learning, and that is good. Recognizing that we are human beings in constant growth is truly exciting!

Emotional regulation is more than just a skill; it's an art. As you master it, you enhance your career and personal life. You can become a beacon of resilience and strength. Recognizing and leading by example with this skill will carry you far as a leader. Your team will recognize it, your family will embrace it, and you will be happier.

# DISCOVER YOUR MOTIVATION AND YOUR "WHY"

*"Find out who you are and do it on purpose."*

**- Dolly Parton**

Real and lasting motivation is tied to living in **alignment with your core values**. How do we discover those values? It starts with looking at the people you admire, the qualities that inspire you, and reflecting on the moments when you've felt most fulfilled. Your core values are the foundation for every decision you make. They should be at the heart of your personal and professional life.

To discover your motivation and your "why," we recommend starting with this exercise: **define your core values**. Reflect on what truly matters to you, what drives your decisions, and what feels right in your gut. Then, look honestly at your life and see if you're living in alignment with those values.

If not, it's time to make a change. When your actions and values align, real motivation kicks in. It's no longer about external rewards or checking boxes—it's about *living your truth*. And that's where the magic happens!

## What is Your Why?

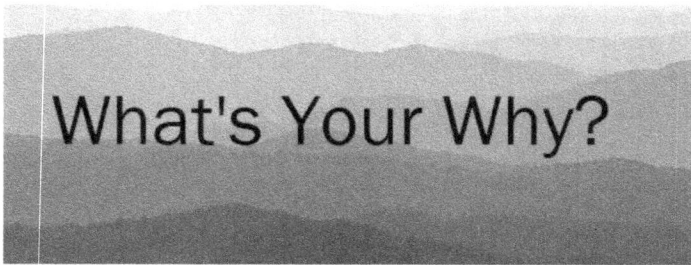

Everything we do in life comes down to one essential question: What is your "why"? What motivates you? What pushes you through the tough times and hurdles you face along the way? The answer is self-motivation. Each of us has a unique "why" that drives us forward.

Tiffany's journey began with the need to survive and provide for her children. That basic need was the spark for everything that followed.

*"I had to feed my kids, so I returned to school. When I became a single mother, I was thrust into a new reality. I had to take charge of my life in a way I never had before. I fought tooth and nail to get into hygiene school. When I finally made it, I encountered barrier after barrier, but I pushed through. My motivation was my kids. I was determined to achieve my goal of earning my hygiene license."*

Everyone has a different motivation driving them; it's important to step back and ask ourselves: What are we striving for? What's the deeper purpose behind the goals we set? When we uncover and identify the real motivations behind our actions, we can push through the inevitable discomfort and challenges that come. That inner drive takes us through the hard times and helps us achieve more than we thought possible."

One key element of motivation is knowing what matters to *you*. Not what society tells you, not someone else's idea of success, but your truth. That's why your story and motivation need to come from within.

Marni recalls, "Growing up in New Jersey, there was this unspoken checklist of things I was supposed to accomplish. I never saw it written down, but it was woven into the culture I grew up in. I was expected to hit certain milestones by a certain age—achieve career success before I was thirty, get married, have a family, and make a certain amount of money. I followed this script without even realizing it, but the truth is, it wasn't my script. It wasn't my "why." I had no idea where these ideas came from, but they dictated my life. I was caught in a current, just going along with the flow."

At twenty-nine years old, I had what I call my "quarter-life" crisis. From the outside, my life looked perfect. I was married to an executive at CBS Sports, had a high-powered job at an advertising agency, and lived in a beautiful apartment on the Upper West Side of Manhattan. But on the inside, I was crumbling. I wasn't living authentically. I wasn't motivated by anything that came from within. I had checked all the boxes, but they weren't *my* boxes. I was living someone else's dream, and it was killing me inside.

That realization hit me hard. I started questioning everything: was it too late to find my "why"? Could I turn things around? I had everything materially, and I wasn't happy. The internal chaos was overwhelming. How could I regulate my emotions when I was disconnected from my truth?

It took me two years to muster the courage to change my life completely. I moved to North Carolina because I saw a life there that felt authentic, something I was missing in New York City. It wasn't easy. It took a lot of self-work—therapy, coaching, books, and facing a mountain of shame. I had to forgive myself for my choices while not living from my center. I had to practice radical acceptance, acknowledging that I had made decisions based on someone else's vision, not mine.

The real work began when I committed to finding *my* "why." It wasn't about feeding others' expectations. It was about aligning my life with my core values and my truth. That's where real motivation starts—when you're honest with yourself about what you truly value and why you're doing what you're doing.

Finding that clarity starts with defining your core values. For me, values like integrity, servant leadership, compassion, vulnerability (with healthy boundaries), and growth became my compass. These are not negotiable. I share them with every client I work with because I want to ensure that we're aligned. I've learned to trust that the right people and opportunities will come into my life when I stay true to these values.

The universe provides when you operate from a place of authenticity and alignment. But we abandon ourselves when we make decisions out of fear, lack of self-motivation, or trying to meet someone else's expectations. And that's the ultimate betrayal. Living a life not aligned with your core values will only drain you from the motivation needed to succeed in the long term. It's not sustainable.

# Your Core Values

So, how can you build a toolkit that includes identifying your core values and finding a supportive community?

Well, consider that we abandon ourselves when we make decisions that go against our core values. This misalignment impacts our self-motivation, especially when focused on long-term success rather than short-term gains. Motivation is deeply connected to how true we are to our values. Once those values are misaligned, things won't flow as smoothly.

It's important to understand that we all have certain values that define us. These values are a baseline for our decisions, actions, and the people we surround ourselves with. For business owners, your guiding principles should reflect your values. Core values should be specific yet have a broad impact. Core values might include honesty, integrity, growth-oriented thinking, teamwork, compassion, accountability, striving for perfection, and attention to detail.

When defining your core values, *less is more*. Focus on a small, essential set of guiding principles. Companies or people will have different values. Think about the people or organizations that inspire you. Write down what you admire about them and how that relates to your values. You might come up with similar terms, like compassion and empathy, but it's useful to dig deeper into the meanings of these words to pinpoint the exact values that resonate with you.

Use the "combine, keep, or kill" method to refine your values further. **Combine** similar values, **keep** the non-negotiable ones, and **kill** (or delete) the ones that don't serve you. This helps create clarity.

**PROTIP:** Take this free quiz
https://datadatabase.wordpress.com/wp-content/uploads/2011/03/schwartz-value-inventory.pdf

We've talked about how selective we are in choosing those who share our values. The success of any client relationship is much greater when values align. Misalignment causes stress and creates obstacles for the company and its team members.

For **Lead 360 Academy**, our virtual on-demand training platform for teams, we've built our core values around professional expertise, approachability, tailored solutions, efficiency in both time and cost, resilience, effectiveness, and, perhaps most importantly, FUN! These principles help ensure that every interaction with teams is grounded in the values we prioritize in our work.

## Staying Motivated

Once you've figured out your core values, the next step is understanding how to stay motivated. There are two types of motivators: internal (intrinsic) and external (extrinsic).

Internal motivators stem from a personal sense of fulfillment—doing something because it brings you satisfaction, joy, or a sense of achievement.

External motivators are based on rewards and punishments, like earning a paycheck, getting a promotion, or avoiding reprimand. Both types of motivation play crucial roles in keeping us on track. Building habits, fostering a growth mindset, and setting rewards for ourselves are practical techniques that keep us motivated.

I had a moment yesterday where I had to finish a client proposal after a long day. I was tired but knew it was important. I used positive self-talk to get through it and promised myself a small reward—a piece of chocolate once I completed it. That mix of intrinsic motivation (getting the work done) and extrinsic motivation (the reward) kept me focused for the next three hours, and I felt accomplished when it was all finished.

I use this approach with my daughter, who's nine years old. We set timers for focused work followed by short breaks, which helps her stay on task and motivated. This teaches her about grit and resilience—key elements of self-motivation. Staying motivated, especially when it's hard or uncomfortable, is about cultivating the ability to push through adversity and build the resilience needed to achieve long-term goals.

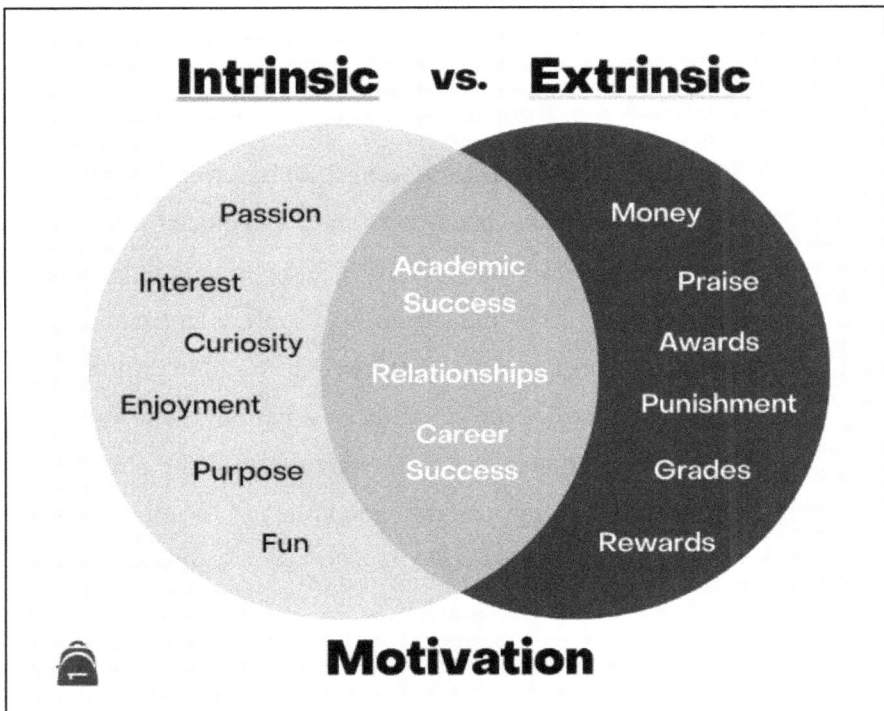

Intrinsic vs. Extrinsic

Passion
Interest
Curiosity
Enjoyment
Purpose
Fun

Academic Success
Relationships
Career Success

Money
Praise
Awards
Punishment
Grades
Rewards

Motivation

## Practical Tips to Stay Motivated

1.  **Set and Track Your Success Metrics**

    Promotions, raises, and recognition are great but are not always in your control. In any case, they don't tell the full story of your accomplishments or worth. Real success isn't limited to external factors. Take ownership by setting your success metrics. At least once a year, step back and reflect on what success looks like for you and how you'll measure it. Start with your personal and professional core values and track your progress regularly. Your metrics should guide your career path. Share your work goals with your boss and ask for specific projects that align with them. Putting yourself in the driver's seat will broaden your perspective on what "success" means, stay motivated, avoid burnout, and build confidence.

2.  **Practice "Right-Spotting"**

    We've spent much time helping teams spot issues and manage risk. That critical lens is useful in business but not so much for happiness. If your work involves problem-solving and you tend to be hard on yourself, try shifting to "right-spotting." Train your brain to focus on what's going well, not just what's wrong. Set an intention to find something positive in every meeting or situation. Invite your team to practice this too—maybe even start meetings by sharing one appreciation. Focusing on the good creates a more positive environment, and your team will benefit just as much as you do.

3.  **Find the Learning**

We are always talking about the importance of learning. We stress it to clients and our kids, even if they sometimes roll their eyes when I ask, "What can we learn from this?" Focusing on learning shifts the energy from disappointment, frustration, or self-criticism to growth and forward movement. Learning strengthens resilience and brings a sense of purpose, boosting your career and happiness. Whether you experience a success or a setback, ask yourself, "What's the lesson here?" and you'll see how it enriches your personal and professional life.

4.  **Build Relationships**

Building strong workplace relationships is one of the most impactful ways to boost happiness and motivation at work. Having friends at work makes a huge difference. Studies show that workplace relationships significantly increase job satisfaction, productivity, and retention. You spend a lot of time at work, so why not enjoy the people you're around? Start by making simple connections—show interest in a coworker, share a bit of yourself, and build from there. A little humor, kindness, and appreciation go a long way. Whether you find a "best friend" at work or create friendly camaraderie, those relationships will make your work life more enjoyable and effective.

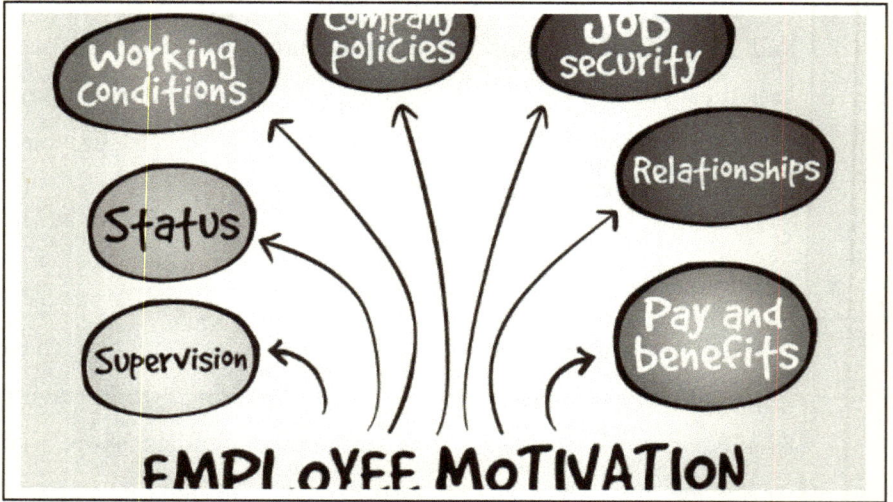

# EMPATHY AND COMPASSION

Tiffany knows this subject all too well…

*"As a provider of care for many years, I deeply felt the emotions of my patients—it was as if I wore their feelings like a suit of armor. The most exhausting part of being a dental hygienist wasn't the job's physical demands but how I would absorb the emotions of those I cared for. We were in close proximity, and I could sense everything: their breathing, body language, and emotions. This constant emotional absorption left me drained by the end of each day, not just physically but emotionally, because I hadn't established healthy boundaries."*

Many medical and dental professionals experience this type of fatigue. It feels almost like a syndrome, where we absorb everything the patient is going through. If they come in anxious or fearful, maybe carrying trauma from childhood dental visits, we feel their reactions, and it can be incredibly exhausting.

This dynamic holds in other areas, too. I've seen friends completely enveloped by what their kids are feeling. It's a natural part of parenting. In the workplace, it's crucial to maintain boundaries. We can still operate with compassion, but we must protect our emotional well-being, especially in the demanding healthcare environments.

Marni had an ah-ha moment while preparing for a "Beginning Mindfulness" lecture. She wanted to discuss the difference between empathy and compassion. There are many definitions of these words, and the most impactful to her was that "compassion is empathy with healthy boundaries."

Compassion is the ability to feel what it is like to walk in someone else's shoes. Empathy is feeling what that person is feeling and getting into their shoes.

For many of us, the word boundaries is like a foreign language. For many empaths, getting into a healthcare profession makes sense because they value helping others. The danger is when you take on others' emotions. You have to be very careful not to experience "empathy fatigue."

## Compassion in Action

There are moments in our professional lives where compassion and emotional intelligence are tested in ways we never anticipated. I attended a case presentation where a man facing double jaw surgery was also recently diagnosed with Hodgkin's lymphoma. It was a heartbreaking and delicate situation. The treatment coordinator was visibly emotional, understanding that recommending palliative care instead of surgery was a compassionate decision given his prognosis.

It was a challenging moment for everyone involved. Emotions ran high. When we work in emotionally charged environments—like healthcare or high-pressure offices—it's easy to take on the emotions of others. The phrase, "This is not mine to hold," serves as a mental boundary. While we may sympathize with someone's pain, we don't have to "carry the weight" of it ourselves.

## Techniques to Help Maintain Emotional Boundaries

Another technique I recommend is envisioning an "energetic bubble" around yourself. This concept is rooted in the scientific fact that we are all made of energy. Walking into a room, we often feel the energy shift—it's not just metaphysical but a biological response. We can absorb others' emotional states, which can be overwhelming. Creating an energetic bubble around ourselves serves as a buffer, helping us stay grounded and protect our emotional well-being.

In a post-pandemic world, emotions in the workplace are more palpable than ever. This heightened emotional climate has resulted in widespread burnout, disengagement, and stress. Gallup's research highlights a worrying trend: employee engagement has dropped from 32% to 17% in recent years.[39] One of the biggest contributors to burnout is the need for more recognition and support from leadership. And it's not just leadership; peer support and acknowledgment are equally powerful in fostering a healthy work environment.

# The Power of Recognition

Recognition, though often underutilized, is one of the simplest yet most impactful tools to address burnout. It costs virtually nothing but has tremendous value. When appreciation is embedded into the weekly workflow, it leads to a culture of gratitude and boosts dopamine levels, which are directly linked to feelings of well-being and joy. In a world where people feel increasingly disconnected, recognition is vital to foster a sense of belonging and connection.

Now more than ever, employees are not just looking for a paycheck; they are searching for workplaces where compassion is part of the organizational DNA. Studies show that employees are willing to work longer hours—or even accept lower pay—for a compassionate employer. Compassion is no longer just a "nice-to-have"; it's a competitive advantage.

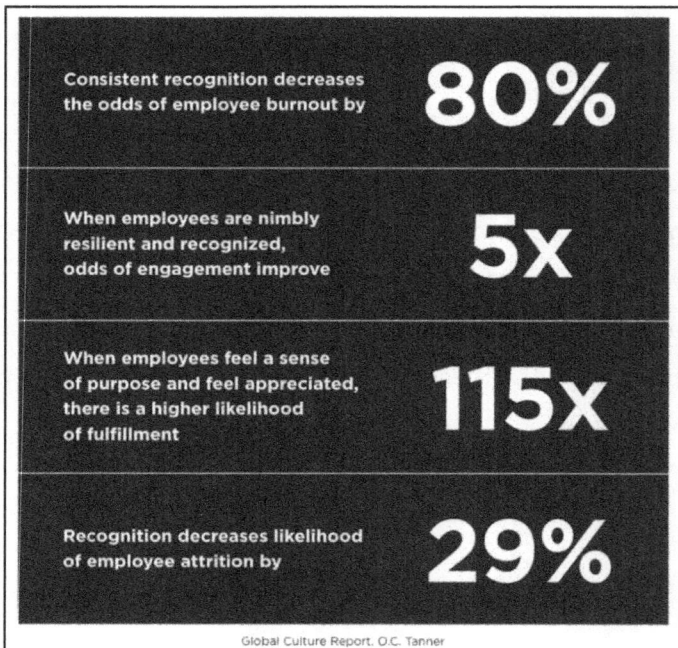

| | |
|---|---|
| Consistent recognition decreases the odds of employee burnout by | **80%** |
| When employees are nimbly resilient and recognized, odds of engagement improve | **5x** |
| When employees feel a sense of purpose and feel appreciated, there is a higher likelihood of fulfillment | **115x** |
| Recognition decreases likelihood of employee attrition by | **29%** |

Global Culture Report. O.C. Tanner

# Creating a Compassionate Workplace Culture

How can leaders and organizations foster a compassionate work culture? It starts with a genuine commitment to understanding employees' needs and emotions. We must ask open-ended questions and listen—to respond and truly understand. Statements like "What I'm hearing you say is…" validate the speaker's emotions and experiences, ensuring they are being heard in a safe, nurturing environment.

Active listening goes beyond hearing words; it involves paying attention to body language, tone of voice, and emotional undercurrents. These conversations enhance the team experience, creating an environment where employees feel valued and understood. This brings us to a critical point: recognizing our own unconscious biases.

We all carry biases shaped by our experiences, upbringing, and cultural background. These biases influence how we communicate and react to others. It's crucial to be aware of the lenses through which we see the world and to set them aside when engaging with others. Doing so allows us to truly understand another person's perspective, allowing for more compassionate communication.

It's important to distinguish between compassion and sympathy. While sympathy involves feeling pity for someone, compassion means putting ourselves in their shoes and truly feeling their emotions. Compassion is the foundation for compassionate action, while sympathy often leaves us on the sidelines, feeling sorry but not necessarily driven to help. This distinction is vital in the workplace, where compassion fuels connection, teamwork, and shared responsibility.

Compassion means being attuned to the emotional well-being of others. I was in a clinical meeting when a young surgical assistant voiced her concern for a struggling new nurse. This simple act of leadership—speaking up for a colleague—demonstrates the power of compassion. Awareness of signs of burnout, such as disengagement or overworking, and checking in with colleagues show that you care.

Compassion doesn't stop at the office door. Employees bring their whole selves to work, and personal challenges can spill into the workplace. Recognizing this and offering support when appropriate can make all the difference. For example, when a staff member shared that her grandmother was in hospice, I made sure to check in on her during my next visit. Sometimes, knowing someone cares is enough to lift a heavy burden.

One of the most beautiful aspects of a compassionate workplace is how it fosters strong team dynamics. When a team member has to step away for personal reasons, the rest of the team steps up, not out of obligation but out of genuine care. This creates a sense of shared responsibility and camaraderie.

Leading with compassion means not just feeling for someone but taking action. If one team member struggles, the rest of the team should step up to support them. This is leadership in action, creating a culture of mutual care and respect. When employees see that their leadership and peers genuinely care about them, they are more likely to stay loyal to the organization and give their best.

Empathy and compassion are not just soft skills; they are THE cornerstones of effective leadership and a thriving workplace culture. By fostering compassion, actively listening, recognizing burnout, and supporting our team members professionally and personally, we create a workplace where everyone feels valued, heard, and supported. This leads to higher engagement, lower turnover, and a more productive, harmonious work environment. Now, more than ever, compassion is the key to building resilient teams and organizations.

# Social Skills

Social skills help us properly manage emotions and connect, interact, and work with others. Empathy is outward-driven; social skills are inward-driven and focus on interacting with and leveraging others to reach our goals.

Building rapport, collaborating effectively, and managing conflict are foundational to success in any professional setting. The ability to win others over (often referred to as "WOO" in CliftonStrengths) is a crucial skill that determines how well individuals and teams work together. Let's delve into how these skills, especially WOO and other social abilities, come into play in everyday interactions and how mastering them can lead to stronger bonds, better cooperation, and improved outcomes.

"Winning Others Over" or WOO, as described in CliftonStrengths, involves the ability to easily persuade, connect, and build relationships. The talent of establishing rapport and creating bonds of trust makes people receptive to your ideas. This is essential, not just in the context of leadership but in any scenario where influencing others is crucial. For example, this skill allows professionals to guide patients toward the best course of action in a dental practice. The aim is never manipulation but rather persuasion rooted in empathy and care for the best outcomes.

Persuading people requires strategy, which needs social skills to be executed effectively. We use our powers of persuasion for good. It's about moving people through their fears, whether a patient hesitates to accept care or a team member resists change. Many decisions, especially around health, are influenced by fear or love. The leader or professional must help people make the right choice through understanding, patience, and clear communication.

Social skills extend far beyond surface-level niceties. At the core, they are about active listening, understanding others, and using emotional intelligence to navigate complex interactions. Dale Carnegie's classic *"How to Win Friends and Influence People"* is a valuable resource that highlights the importance of building relationships and practicing empathy.

Whether in dentistry, medical settings, or business, social skills are not just taught; they are developed. Every interaction provides an opportunity to improve these skills. For instance, starting conversations can feel awkward, but learning to initiate meaningful dialogue is crucial. Whether speaking to a patient about their health concerns or navigating a tense meeting at work, it is invaluable to put people at ease and make them feel understood.

Nonverbal communication also plays a huge role. Reading body language, tone of voice, and subtle cues can inform how you respond in the moment. This is especially true in healthcare settings where patients may not always express their concerns verbally, but their body language or facial expressions can communicate discomfort, fear, or uncertainty. Attention to these nonverbal signals allows professionals to provide better care and build trust with patients or clients.

**KEY ELEMENTS TO HELP BUILD TEAMWORK IN THE OFFICE:**

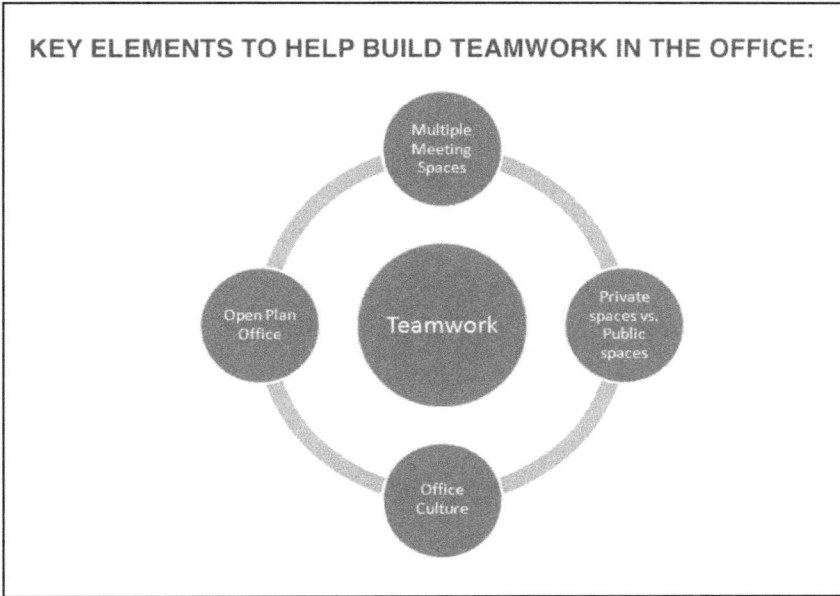

Strong social skills also enable collaboration. Effective teams happen when each member feels heard, understood, and valued. As a leader or team member, listening and considering others' perspectives is crucial for achieving common goals. The power of collaboration is in its ability to bring out the best in people, harnessing their unique talents and contributions for the collective good.

Collaboration is not just beneficial—it's necessary. In dental schools, professionals learn the importance of teamwork when treating patients. As they transition into practice, those skills evolve and translate into fostering cooperative work environments.

Building rapport and bonds within the team is fundamental in any business. These bonds are the foundation of a strong organizational culture, where every individual feels connected to the company's core values, mission, and goals.

Consider the construction of a house. The foundation of a house—or your business—begins with the leadership team. Their actions and decisions lay the groundwork for the rest of the organization.

Core values are the "blueprint" for how everyone works together. Transparency, collaboration, and excellence guide the team's actions and interactions. When teams unite to establish these values through mission statement exercises or other collaborative projects, they build a sense of ownership, mutual respect, and understanding.

Building rapport isn't just reserved for colleagues—it's equally important when interacting with customers. Establishing rapport is about connecting through shared experiences or simply making the other person feel heard and understood.

Establishing rapport with patients is crucial in healthcare, particularly dental practices. Patients are often nervous, apprehensive, or even fearful of procedures. Creating an environment of trust and comfort is essential. Small talk, asking about their interests, or relating to their background helps break down barriers and create a more relaxed atmosphere. Simple gestures, like smiling, maintaining eye contact, and listening attentively, can make a difference in a patient's experience.

This rapport-building process is not just about immediate care; it's about creating long-term relationships. When patients feel a connection with their dentist, they are more likely to stay loyal to the practice, trust recommendations, and refer others.

Mastering social skills—whether through WOO, active listening, or conflict management—paves the way for success in any business or healthcare setting. These skills build strong teams, foster collaboration, and create lasting bonds with patients or clients. As you continue to learn and refine these abilities, you enhance your ability to lead, communicate, and positively influence those around you.

Businesses and practices prioritizing social skills see better outcomes through improved patient care, stronger team dynamics, or increased customer satisfaction. It's about using the power of connection and persuasion for the greater good, always moving people toward the best possible outcomes.

# SECTION III
## COMMUNICATION

# COMMUNICATION

"*Great leaders communicate, and great communicators lead.*"

– **Simon Sinek**

## Tiffany's Story

During my high school basketball days, one unforgettable incident underscored the importance of communication in team sports. We were in a heated game, and I struggled with a particular play. Unfortunately, our team was not communicating effectively. This set the stage for an accident. The point guard called out a play, but her voice didn't carry across the court, and she failed to use the code word we had practiced. This caused a ripple of confusion among us. As I sprinted down the court, ready to assume my position, I realized too late we were not on the same page.

The miscommunication led to a disastrous outcome—my point guard launched the ball down the court, aiming for a teammate who wasn't where she expected. Instead, the ball struck me on the head, knocking me out momentarily. After regaining my senses and being helped off the court by the trainers, our coach expressed his disappointment. He emphasized the vital role of communication in our game, scolding us for not listening to each other. I was left with a throbbing headache and a strong sense of embarrassment. However, this painful experience taught me an invaluable lesson about the power of clear communication.

It became clear that we could have avoided the misstep with effective communication. If the point guard had clearly articulated the play and if we had been actively listening and responding, the game might have unfolded differently. This incident reinforced the notion that communication is about more than just speaking. Effective communication means ensuring messages are conveyed and understood. This realization not only transformed my approach to teamwork in sports but also instilled a lifelong appreciation for the role of communication in achieving success, both on and off the court.

### How Do You Communicate?

The third pillar in successful businesses and people involves practicing and promoting great communication. Communication is exchanging information, ideas, and emotions between individuals or groups. Well-developed communication enriches our professional and personal lives. Practicing these communication skills can lead to remarkable achievements in any business setting. Effective communication bridges gaps between departments and enhances collaboration, driving innovation and progress. The foundation of these skills begins when we learn to express thoughts and emotions as children.

Over time, these abilities are honed and refined to fit the nuances of professional environments. As individuals continue to refine their communication skills, they experience transformative personal and professional growth. Mastering communication can enhance leadership capabilities, strengthen relationships, and create a more cohesive organizational culture. Effective communication is a powerful tool that can propel businesses and individuals toward greater success.

Communication is about creating verbal and non-verbal connections. It's about giving and receiving feedback in a way that fosters growth, collaboration, and understanding. Whether it's a quick check-in during a meeting or an in-depth performance review, how we communicate impacts our relationships and success. Next time you're engaging with someone, remember: **it's not just about what you say, but how you say it—and what you're willing to hear in return.**

### The Benefits of Effective Communication

Communication in the workplace is a cornerstone of success. Effective communication fosters team collaboration, efficiency, and a positive work environment. Communication promotes exchanging ideas, feedback, and information, enabling teams to work cohesively towards shared goals. By promoting open dialogue, communication helps to create a clearer direction and focus. Good communication helps define roles, establish clear expectations, and align efforts, boosting overall productivity and efficiency.

Effective communication is crucial for informed decision-making. When team members voice their insights and concerns, improved discussions lead to better solutions. Inclusive communication also boosts employee engagement, as individuals feel valued and heard, leading to higher motivation and retention.

Team members who can communicate freely are happier employees. When leadership promotes and nurtures effective communication, the business benefits. I often ask long-term employees about what keeps them engaged. Interestingly, their responses rarely focus on financial incentives.

Instead, they emphasize the **positive company culture and effective communication**, which make them feel valued and satisfied. Long-term employees bring experience, stability, and a deep understanding of business processes. Good communication in the workplace enhances team culture, creates a positive atmosphere, and significantly boosts customer satisfaction.

Strong communication skills are equally vital for building and maintaining robust customer relationships. Clear, empathetic interactions with clients or customers foster trust, enhance satisfaction, and encourage loyalty. By actively listening to customer feedback, businesses can adapt and innovate based on real-world needs, reinforcing their competitive position.

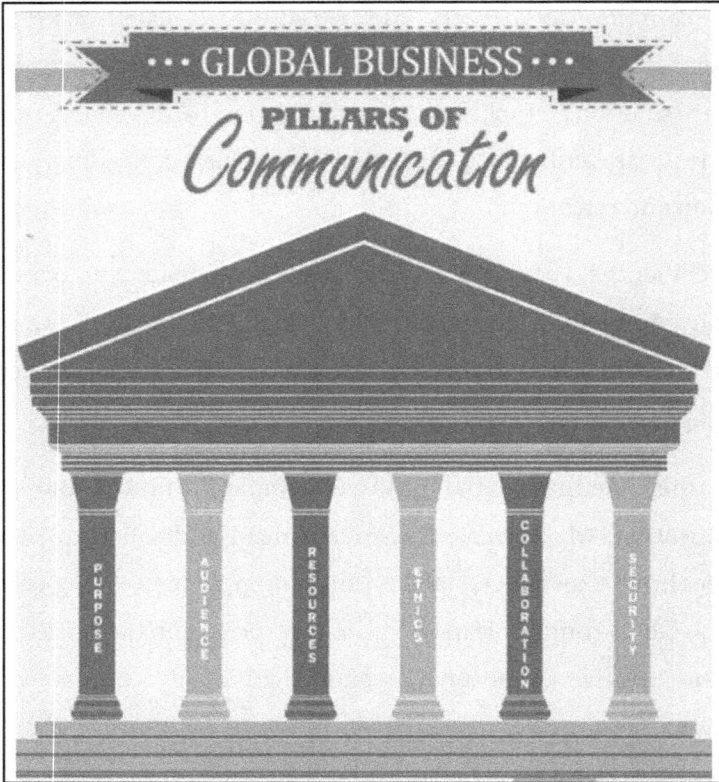

Communication also plays a critical role in conflict management. By ensuring that messages are clear and consistent, organizations can reduce the potential for errors and misinterpretations that lead to disputes. When conflicts do arise, effective communication helps resolve them swiftly, maintaining a harmonious workplace.

As businesses evolve, so must their communication strategies. Effective communication supports organizational growth by enabling adaptability. Clear communication helps guide teams through transitions in times of change, ensuring everyone is informed and aligned with new directions or initiatives. Howard Schultz, the visionary behind Starbucks, demonstrated the profound impact of effective communication on business success.

Schultz, who returned as CEO in 2008 during a turbulent time for the company, exemplified how transparent and empathetic communication could turn around a struggling business. One of Schultz's notable communication strategies was his emphasis on **transparency and direct engagement with employees**, whom he called "partners." Understanding the value of their contribution, Schultz organized open forums and town hall meetings, inviting partners to share their insights and concerns. This approach made employees feel heard and valued. They provided Schultz with firsthand perspectives that were crucial for making informed decisions.

A key demonstration of Schultz's communication prowess came during the 2008 financial crisis. Starbucks faced declining sales and the need to close numerous stores. Instead of shying away, Schultz addressed the situation head-on. He communicated candidly with partners and investors, outlining the challenges and his strategic vision for revitalizing the brand. His straightforward, compassionate communication instilled confidence and rallied the workforce toward a common goal.

Schultz demonstrated good communication by fostering a culture of open dialogue. He encouraged feedback at all levels and was known for his accessibility. This openness cultivated a sense of belonging and ownership among partners, motivating them to contribute to the company's success.

The results of Schultz's leadership were evident. Starbucks recovered and thrived, expanding its global footprint and innovating in the coffee industry. Schultz's ability to communicate was a cornerstone of his leadership. He proved that communication is crucial to building a successful and resilient business. Through his example, Schultz showed that clear, empathetic, and inclusive communication can transform a company and lay the foundation for lasting success.

Most great leaders excel in communication; communication is key to running a team effectively. Clear, open, consistent communication is crucial for achieving business goals. It lays the groundwork for a collaborative, efficient, and adaptable organization, ensuring long-term success in a competitive environment. It can also create a cohesive work environment, fostering collaboration and driving organizational success.

Let's take a deep approach and discuss the four types of communication. These include verbal, written, nonverbal, and visual communication.

## Communication Styles

So, how do you communicate? Understanding how you and the people around you communicate is key to understanding and clarity. Find a free quiz now: www.CultureCatalystBook.com/quizzes

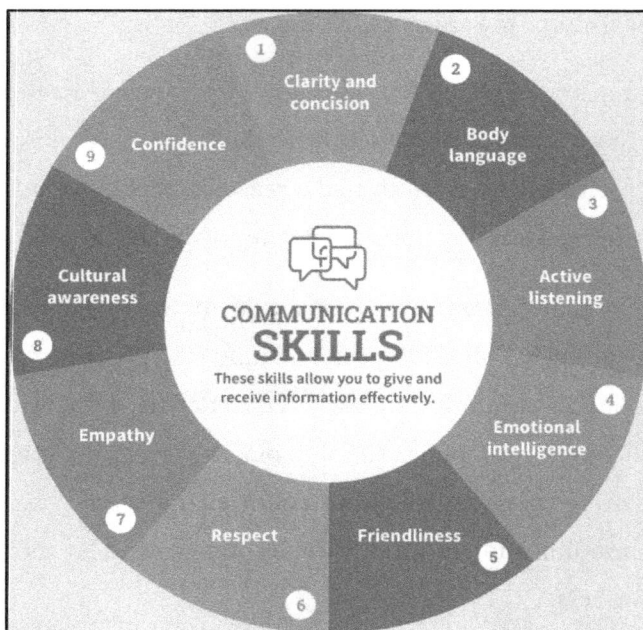

# The Four Quadrant Styles

- Associators and Innovators are primarily concerned with relationships.
- For Associators, it's mostly relationships among people
- Innovators think of relationships of ideas and how they relate to people.
- Systemizers and Energizers look at results—data and then deliverables.

**Style 1: Energizer: Direct/Fast-Paced, Results Oriented**

- Characteristics: Pragmatic, Direct, Impatient, Decisive, Quick, Energetic
- Discussion Topics: Results, Objectives, Performance, Efficiency, Progress, Decisions,
- Responsibility, Feedback, Achievements
- Priorities: Action, Accomplishment
- Time: Right now

Skills: Highly productive, energetic, enthusiastic, good at making decisions

Weaknesses: May come across as Impatient, insensitive, and missing details

Communicating with an Energizer

- Brevity is key; talk in bullet points
- Focus on results first
- Emphasize the practicality of the idea
- Make direct eye contact and be confident
- Use visual aids
- Walk and talk

**Style 2: Systemizer: Indirect/Slow Paced, Results Oriented**

- Characteristics: Logical, Analytical, Organized, Systematic, Factual, Cautious
- Discussion Topics: Facts, Procedures, Planning, Organizing, Controlling, Testing, Trying things
- out, Analysis, Observations, Proof, Details
- Priorities: Facts, Order, Details
- Time: Past, Present, and Future
- Skills: Organize information well, less prone to mistakes
- Weaknesses: May come across as picky, aloof, critical

Communicating with a Systemizer

- Focus on facts and data
- Provide proof and methodology to back up the proposal
- Keep discussion/proposal in logical order (background, current situation, results)
- Provide written documentation
- Do not rush

**Style 3: Associator: Indirect/Slow Paced, Relationship Oriented**

- Characteristics: Friendly, Warm, Empathetic, Emotional, Perceptive, Sensitive, Spontaneous
- Discussion Topics: People Needs, Motivation, Teamwork, Communication, Feelings, Self-
- Development, Awareness, Relationships
- Priorities: Relationships, People

- Time: Past
- Skills: Perceptive, friendly, team players
- Weaknesses: May come across as Unassertive, emotional, slow

Communicating with an Associator

- Allow for personal talk, build rapport
- Connect results to relationships and people
- Seek their opinions/ideas
- Discuss past results and successes

**Style 4: Innovator: Direct/Fast Paced, Relationship Oriented**

- Characteristics: Charismatic, Creative, Difficult to Understand, Full of Ideas, Provocative
- Discussion Topics: Concepts, Innovation, New Ways, New Methods, Improvement, New Ideas,
- Opportunities, Possibilities, Big Picture, Potential
- Priorities: Relationships, People
- Time: Future
- Skills: Visionary, Creative, See the big picture
- Weaknesses: May come across as difficult to understand, unrealistic, unproductive

Communicating with an Innovator

- Allow time for brainstorming
- Talk about the big picture and what the idea could mean
- Stress the uniqueness of an idea or topic
- Follow-up meeting with brief to-do list

## Verbal Communication

It was a typical Monday morning at the office, and Mike was late. Stumbling into the breakroom, bleary-eyed, he spotted his colleague, Sarah, brewing coffee. He sighed in relief.

"Sarah, could you do me a huge favor and grab me a cup of coffee when it's ready?" Mike mumbled, mid-yawn.

"No problem," Sarah replied, barely glancing up from her phone. She was scrolling through dog memes while waiting for the coffee to finish.

As Mike stumbled to his desk, he shot Sarah a thumbs-up. "Thanks! I need it, black, no sugar!"

Unfortunately, Sarah was already back to watching a TikTok video about organizing kitchen drawers. She heard Mike talking but didn't catch the specifics. Black, no sugar? Or maybe he said milk and extra sugar?

20 minutes later...

Mike practically vibrated from caffeine withdrawal as Sarah finally came over with a cup. Grinning, she handed it over.

"Here you go! One coffee, just like you asked!" she beamed.

Mike eagerly took a big sip—and instantly gagged.

"What... what is this?" he spat.

"Coffee with milk and extra sugar, just like you said!" Sarah replied confidently.

"Nooo! I said black, no sugar!" Mike exclaimed, wiping his mouth like he'd just eaten a lemon.

"Oh... whoops," Sarah said sheepishly. "I thought you said extra sugar. My bad."

Mike sighed and rubbed his temples. "Alright, no big deal. I'll get it myself. Can you handle that email to the client about the pricing update?"

Sarah, still trying to redeem herself, nodded enthusiastically. "Got it! I'll let them know we'll lower the price by 15%."

Mike stopped dead in his tracks. "Wait… no, we're raising the price by 15%. Sarah, did you even hear what I said?"

"Ohhhh… you know what, I was still thinking about the coffee situation," she admitted, chuckling awkwardly.

Fast forward to the afternoon…

The client was very confused. In one email, they were told the price was going down. A second immediately claimed the price was going up. A third email, which tried to clarify things, added more confusion when Sarah accidentally sent a GIF of a dancing banana.

Mike finally decided to step in. "Alright, Sarah, we need to talk. We're missing each other here."

"Agreed," Sarah said, scratching her head. "I'll be honest; I'm still stuck on the coffee thing."

So, what is the moral of the story? Miscommunication can turn a simple request for coffee into a caffeine catastrophe and a pricing update into a client circus. Always double-check what's being said—coffee orders or client emails—because things can get wonky fast when we're not on the same page!

\* \* \*

NEW YORK TIMES BESTSELLER

**Douglas Stone & Sheila Heen**

*of the Harvard Negotiation Project and coauthors of*

DIFFICULT CONVERSATIONS

# Thanks for the Feedback

THE SCIENCE AND ART OF
RECEIVING FEEDBACK WELL*

*even when it is off base, unfair, poorly delivered,
and, frankly, you're not in the mood*

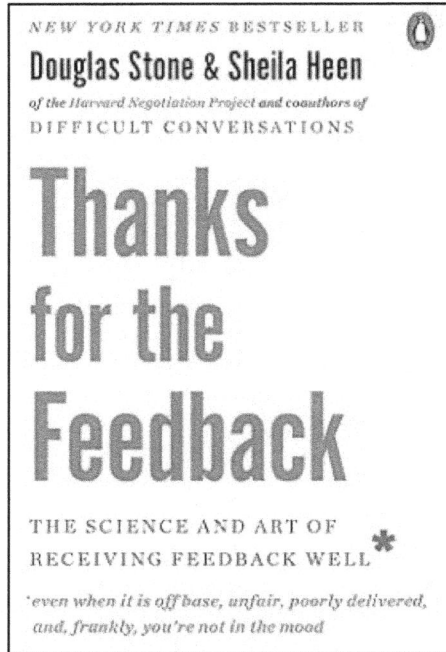

## Verbal Vs. Non-Verbal Communication

Verbal communication encompasses all speech-based interactions between individuals, including spoken words, written messages, and sign language. The primary distinction between verbal and non-verbal communication is using words to convey messages. It refers to all speech-based communication between two or more people, including spoken words, written messages, and sign language.

Verbal communication is crucial in the workplace, significantly impacting team dynamics. Effective verbal communication fosters collaboration, trust, and productivity by ensuring all team members are on the same page. Clear communication minimizes misunderstandings and conflicts, creating a harmonious work environment. This clarity enables team members to collaborate more effectively, leverage each other's strengths, and work towards common goals with a unified approach. Verbal communication facilitates instant feedback and idea sharing, which can drive innovative solutions and enhance team performance.

I witnessed this firsthand in 2021 while working with a large team. This business, consisting of numerous team members, recognized the critical importance of exceptional communication. I was truly impressed by the exceptional communication skills demonstrated by the twenty-three team members. Typically, seventeen staff members were on duty each day.

To ensure precise communication, we implemented a headset and code system to streamline business processes in real time. This allowed the team to relay information quickly, ensuring that every member was fully informed about the progress and status of each situation and customer interaction at every step.

Verbal communication is a powerful tool in leadership for inspiring, guiding, and aligning teams with organizational objectives. Great leaders communicate verbally to articulate a clear vision, set expectations, and motivate their teams. By engaging in open dialogues, leaders can foster a culture of trust and respect, encouraging team members to share their thoughts and concerns.

**Tools For Effective Verbal Communication**

**Active Listening**

Active listening is a key component of effective verbal communication. It allows leaders to understand their team's needs and provide constructive feedback. This strengthens relationships and empowers team members to contribute their best, driving the organization toward long-term success.

### Awareness

You can't be aware of how you communicate unless you are in the present moment. This means monitoring your headspace to avoid living in an imagined future or the past. Practice being present to be more aware. Once you are aware of this, you can notice repeated communication challenges. Start by being curious about the patterns. Curiosity is a neutral, non-judgmental emotion that allows us to explore without beating ourselves up. It helps uncover whether the issue lies in verbal, non-verbal, written, or visual communication so we can adapt accordingly.

### Avoid the Word "But"

Did you know that using the word "but" negates everything you said before it? For example, "I want to thank you so much for everything you are doing here for me at this office, **but** I need to talk to you about an issue I'm having." By using the word "but," you completely remove the compliment. Now, the person is focused only on what comes *after* the but. Try this approach: "Thank you so much for everything you do for me here at this office. I would appreciate the opportunity to talk with you about an issue I'm having." Do you see the difference? Avoid the "but" at all costs!

### KISS - Keep it Simple, Sweetheart

Communication is often about simplifying. We can learn from children. Watching kids live in the moment, filled with joy, reminds us of the power of simplicity. Good communication follows the same principle—be clear, say what you mean, and don't hesitate to ask questions. As Paul Derby from Derby Communications suggests, *"Speak like a normal person, make it real, tell a story, and listen more."* [40] This keeps your communication engaging and meaningful.

You'll connect with your audience more effectively by keeping things simple and asking the right questions.

## Avoid Cognitive Distress

Cognitive distress occurs when we overload someone's brain with too much information. A Harvard Business Review article [41]discusses this concept, emphasizing the importance of delivering messages simply. When teaching new concepts, imagine explaining them to a ten-year-old. By simplifying the information, you show kindness and prevent cognitive overload. This principle applies whether you're presenting complex ideas to teams, communicating with patients, or interacting with customers. Breaking down processes into easy-to-understand steps allows for greater impact.

## Anchoring

Another key element of effective communication is anchoring new information to something the audience already understands. For instance, Warren Buffett uses the analogy of moats and castles to explain the complex concept of protecting a company from competitors. This relatable metaphor helps people grasp an otherwise intricate business strategy. Using analogies like this, especially in medical or health fields, can make complicated ideas more accessible.

### 7 Tips for Overcoming Workplace Communication Challenges

| 1 | 2 | 3 | 4 |
|---|---|---|---|
| Set Clear Expectations | Seek Feedback | Ask for Clarification | Implement Communication Tools |

| 5 | 6 | 7 |
|---|---|---|
| Be Clear and Listen Actively | Avoid Assumptions | Use Nonverbal Clues |

Hermann

**Use a Framework**

A great framework for prioritizing communication is based on three simple questions:

*What? So what? Now what?*

- *What* defines the facts, situation, product, or position? This sets the foundation by explaining the key details.
- *So, What* addresses why this information is important to your audience, making it relevant to them?
- *Now What* outlines the next steps or a call to action, such as taking questions or setting up a follow-up meeting.

This flexible structure is a powerful tool for more effective communication. Whether presenting an idea, leading a meeting, or answering questions, this framework helps you keep things clear and focused.

## Receiving and Giving Feedback

*"It takes humility to seek feedback. It takes wisdom to understand it, analyze it, and appropriately act on it."*—**Stephen Covey**

We often think of feedback as negative, something to endure. Feedback is a gift and comes in many forms—some subtle, some overt. I love a great book called *Thanks for the Feedback: The Science and Art of Receiving Feedback Well* by Douglas Stone and Sheila Heen. It emphasizes how we're constantly swimming in an ocean of feedback, whether it's performance reviews at work, responses to emails, or even the SAT scores kids receive in school.

In the workplace, good feedback guides our actions to:

- Self-regulate and respond to inner and outer expectations.
- Maintain perspective about what's valuable to accomplish.

- Connect individual aspirations with company goals.
- Create a sense of belonging to a tribe…or a team.
- Increase intrinsic motivation and, as a result, performance.

Feedback is information about how someone is doing to reach a particular set of goals. It comes in at least three formats:

- **Appreciation**: Recognizing and rewarding someone for great work. Appreciation connects and motivates people, and it's vital since intrinsic motivation is one of the critical factors for high performance.
- **Coaching**: Helping someone expand their knowledge, skills, and capabilities. Coaching is also an opportunity to address feelings, which helps balance and strengthen relationships.
- **Evaluation**: Assessing someone against a set of standards, aligning expectations, and informing decision-making.

Many struggle with receiving feedback well. Some people respond defensively, making it difficult to create a culture of growth. I emphasize the importance of framing feedback in a supportive way. Instead of focusing on what someone is doing wrong, I frame it as an *opportunity for growth*. This creates an environment where the person receiving the feedback feels nurtured and valued rather than attacked.

**Feedback Frameworks:**

*The Compliment Sandwich*

Use a compliment sandwich technique when delivering coaching or evaluation feedback. Start with a compliment (like the bread), insert the coaching or evaluation feedback (the meat), then end with a compliment (more bread).

*The Pit Stop*

Use for both one-to-one reviews and evaluations

*One to Ones*

1. Establish rapport.

   - **How are you?**
   - And how is your family?
   - How are things at work?
2. Make people mindful of today.
   - What's on your mind today?
   - And what else?
   - How can I help you? Is there anything I can do for you?
3. Appreciate, Coach, or Evaluate.
   - Make explicitly clear which one it is.

Misunderstanding the type of feedback being given is where communication often breaks down. For example, you might be looking for constructive coaching, but all you get is a pat on the back, or vice versa. Understanding this distinction helps us become better communicators in giving and receiving feedback.

Remember, feedback goes both up and down the org chart. Teams need to give regular feedback to leadership, and leadership needs to give regular feedback to the team!

*Keep In Mind...*

Receiving feedback, whether appreciation, coaching, or evaluation, doesn't mean you have to accept or act on every piece of advice you get. It's more about maintaining an openness to listen and practicing a growth mindset.

*Just because you're listening doesn't mean you're obligated
to make their input your own.*

It means showing respect by being open to hearing what they say. This isn't easy—our instincts are often defensive. We're wired for survival; feedback can feel like an attack. Mindfulness is key. When receiving feedback, we must be fully present and aware of how we react.

A simple yet powerful tip is to focus on your breathing. Let your breath anchor you to engage in active listening fully. During feedback, nod your head and use body language; resist the urge to respond immediately. Let the feedback sink in before making any judgments or decisions. Receiving feedback well means engaging thoughtfully and deciding what to do with the information later, not in the heat of the moment.

Feedback often triggers emotional responses; being aware of these triggers helps you manage them. The key is seeing yourself from another perspective—without this openness, growth stalls. It's a difficult skill to master but incredibly rewarding. We all have blind spots; addressing them improves personal and professional relationships. Communication gets muddled because we're unaware of these blind spots. Feedback, if approached well, helps us clear that up.

We all have our strengths and weaknesses, but it's essential to communicate feedback in a way that supports growth. Doing this with kindness and intention fosters a sense of psychological safety, allowing for deeper connections and better outcomes in the workplace.

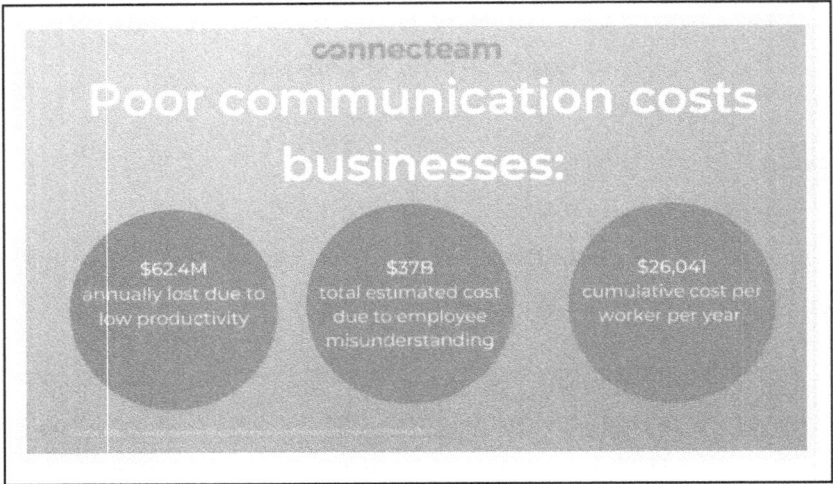

## Common Communication Challenges in the Workplace

1.  ### Direct Communication is Key

    A common issue I see in workplaces is people sidestepping direct communication. Recently, one of my front desk employees came to me. The employee was concerned that the treatment coordinator was investigating an issue and might blame him. Instead of addressing his concern directly with her, he came to us. My advice was simple: "Why don't you take her to a private room and have an open conversation?" Using "I feel" statements, such as "I feel concerned because it seems like you're investigating this situation and I want to make sure we're on the same page," allows for a courageous and constructive dialogue.

    **SOLUTION:** Direct communication is critical, especially when tensions or misunderstandings arise. Instead of talking behind people's backs, go straight to the source. That's how real communication happens.

2.  **Passive Aggressive Communication**

Passive-aggressive communication involves expressing negative feelings or thoughts indirectly, often concealing hostility behind a facade of politeness.[42]

Passive-aggressive behavior is rooted in complex emotions and interpersonal dynamics, such as fear of losing control, insecurity, or lack of self-esteem. Some individuals use passive-aggressive behavior as a coping mechanism in response to stress, anxiety, or dealing with conflict or rejection. Individuals sometimes engage in passive-aggressive behavior because they harbor grudges or feel underappreciated or undervalued.[43]

Passive-aggressive communication manifests in various ways. It can involve sarcasm, subtle insults, backhanded compliments, the silent treatment, or even deliberate forgetfulness. [44] Passive-aggressive individuals often avoid confrontation and hide their true feelings, making it difficult to address and resolve underlying issues.

Common passive-aggressive phrases include, "I wouldn't expect you to understand," "That's a big accomplishment, especially for you," or "I guess it must be nice always to have so much free time for yourself." These phrases seem positive but carry an underlying tone of criticism. Passive aggression often leads to negative interaction patterns and breakdowns in effective communication between individuals.

**SOLUTION:** When you see someone engaging in passive-aggressive communication, call it out gently by talking with them privately. Explain to them what they are doing and how it makes others feel. Ask them to be more aware of how they interact.

3. **Ego and Attitude**

The ego can be tricky to maneuver in the workplace. Some team members may want to step over or talk over each other, while others may never want to back down from winning an argument. Often, people refuse to accept that they are part of the problem, which can lead to resentment, misunderstanding, and discomfort.

**SOLUTION:** An accountability chart clearly defining roles and responsibilities is extremely helpful. Investing in conflict management and other "soft skills" training from a trusted outside source can also help. We will discuss conflict resolution tools in this chapter to help further explain.

4. **Information** *Overload*

The "tech stack" in many offices is overwhelming. Managing Slack, your project management system, texts, emails, calls, and many other systems teams can be challenging. Important communication can get lost in all the "noise."

**SOLUTION:** Create a formal communication guidelines manifesto that outlines what gets communicated where, when, and how. For example, in one of my client's practices, we only use Slack for urgent and important messages. We use email for non-urgent items that are still important.

## Generational Communication Gaps

Organizations in today's workforce often manage teams spanning multiple generations. From seasoned Baby Boomers to ambitious Millennials and the rising Generation Z, the workplace is a melting pot of varying perspectives, experiences, and expectations.

Recently, I became aware of the importance of minimizing what "mainstream" cultural references are when I present or have discussions. For example, I was presenting to a group of younger hygienists and referred to something I thought was funny. Crickets ensued. I used one of my classics... a reference to the movie, "Ferris Bueller," where the professor repeatedly calls out Ferris's name as no one responds. The problem here? No one got my reference. Oops. I realized that I have become the "older" person here... which inevitably happens to all of us. Another reference? I was sitting with a potential new team member and the business manager. Both men are in their early thirties. I was discussing that we have a strict policy on no toxicity in the workplace. I said, "Homey, don't play that," referring to the 1990's show, "In Living Color." They had no idea what I was referencing! Lesson learned!

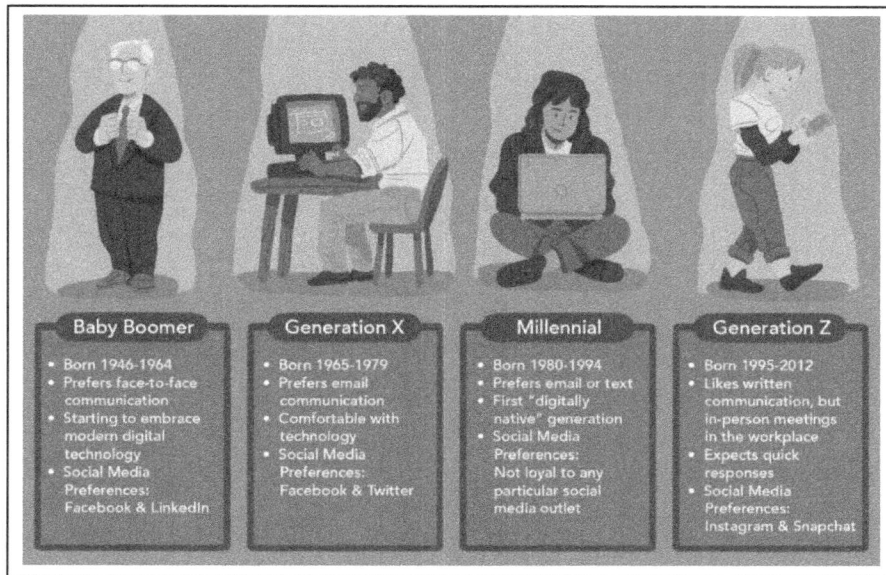

| Baby Boomer | Generation X | Millennial | Generation Z |
|---|---|---|---|
| • Born 1946-1964 | • Born 1965-1979 | • Born 1980-1994 | • Born 1995-2012 |
| • Prefers face-to-face communication | • Prefers email communication | • Prefers email or text | • Likes written communication, but in-person meetings |
| • Starting to embrace modern digital technology | • Comfortable with technology | • First "digitally native" generation | in the workplace |
| • Social Media Preferences: Facebook & LinkedIn | • Social Media Preferences: Facebook & Twitter | • Social Media Preferences: Not loyal to any particular social media outlet | • Expects quick responses • Social Media Preferences: Instagram & Snapchat |

**Workplace Communication Preferences Across Generations**

Communication in the workplace can look very different depending on generational backgrounds. Each generation's unique experiences shape their communication style. Understanding these differences is key to effective teamwork and leadership.

Here's a breakdown of communication styles across generations and how they impact workplace dynamics:

*Baby Boomers (Born 1946–1964)*

Baby Boomers are known for their optimism, competitiveness, and strong work ethic. Events like the Vietnam War, the Civil Rights Movement, and Watergate shaped their formative years. They value loyalty, teamwork, and duty. Regarding communication, efficiency is key; they're comfortable with phone calls and face-to-face interactions.

*Generation X (Born 1965–1980)*

Generation X tends to be flexible and independent and values work-life balance. Growing up during events like the AIDS epidemic, the fall of the Berlin Wall, and the rise of the dot-com boom, they focus on personal and professional interests over company loyalty. Like Boomers, they appreciate efficient communication, whether it's through phone calls or in-person meetings.

*Millennials (Born 1981–2000)*

Millennials are known for their civic-mindedness and openness to diversity. Events like 9/11, Columbine, and the explosion of the internet have shaped their worldviews. They value responsibility, leadership quality, and unique work experiences. When communicating, they often prefer instant messaging, emails, and texts.

*Generation Z (Born 2001–2020)*

Gen Z is entrepreneurial, global-minded, and values diversity and creativity. Raised during the aftermath of 9/11 and the Great Recession, they've been surrounded by technology their whole lives. They prefer instant messaging, texts, and social media, favoring quick, informal communication.

Managers who understand these differences can foster better collaboration, creating a workplace that respects and leverages each generation's strengths.

## Fostering an Open Communication Culture

Encourage open dialogue about communication preferences. Each generation has its preferences for how they communicate, whether face-to-face, over the phone, via email, or through messaging apps. By fostering a culture of open communication, you can ensure everyone's preferences are respected and understood.

Leaders often encounter challenges that stem from communication failures. These can be effectively addressed by fostering an open communication culture. By encouraging transparent dialogue, leaders can bridge gaps and build trust within the team. Implementing regular feedback sessions helps identify and resolve issues early, while effective communication ensures messages are accurately conveyed.

Active listening is crucial, as it demonstrates genuine interest in team members' perspectives, making them feel valued and heard. Creating an environment where employees are comfortable expressing their thoughts and concerns leads to a more cohesive, collaborative team, ultimately enhancing overall performance. A monthly team meeting schedule can help avert numerous issues by encouraging active verbal communication.

Consistent monthly team meetings foster effective communication within and across a company. These regular gatherings enhance collaboration by ensuring everyone is aligned on goals and objectives. They provide a dedicated platform for addressing concerns, sharing updates, and celebrating successes. By adopting this practice, businesses often see improved performance and heightened team morale. Employees feel more informed, valued, and engaged with their work.

I currently work with a business, prioritizing monthly meetings to discuss new and ongoing goals and projects. During these meetings, they reflect on the company's mission statement, reaffirm their purpose, and explore ways to serve their customers best. Since adopting this approach, the business has experienced significant growth and success. The company culture is outstanding, as every team member feels confident and secure in understanding the company's direction.

The leadership team guides these meetings with a well-defined agenda, ensuring they are consistently productive and focused. Team members provide feedback, contributing to a positive and effective outcome.

Implementing this approach in your business can lead to transformative changes by enhancing communication between leadership and the team. Besides verbal communication, written communication promotes clarity, effective record-keeping, and accessibility, allowing complex information to be conveyed efficiently. It supports collaboration by ensuring all team members are aligned and have a reference point for future discussions.

How can you improve communication between management and employees

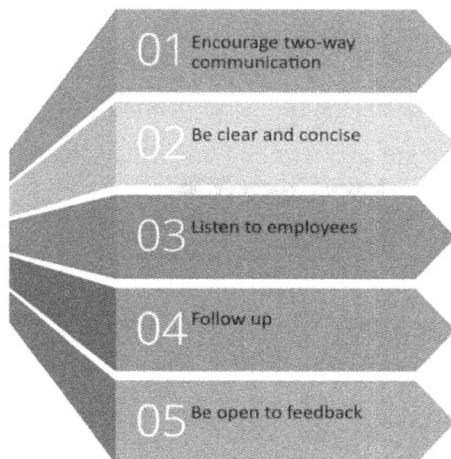

01 Encourage two-way communication

02 Be clear and concise

03 Listen to employees

04 Follow up

05 Be open to feedback

# Power of Written Communication

Founded by Jeff Bezos in 1994, Amazon has grown into a behemoth in e-commerce, cloud computing, and more, largely due to its unique communication strategies. One of the signature practices at Amazon is the use of detailed written memos. Bezos implemented this approach to ensure that ideas and strategies are thoroughly thought-out and articulated. Each memo is in a narrative format, usually six pages long, and is read silently at the beginning of meetings. This practice encourages deep thinking and clarity, allowing for more productive discussions and decision-making.

Internally, written communication is also pivotal in Amazon's famous "two-pizza teams," small, autonomous teams that operate with minimal bureaucracy. These teams are encouraged to maintain detailed project and progress records through written reports and documentation. This ensures that knowledge is shared across the company, reducing silos and enhancing collaboration.

Additionally, Amazon uses written communication to maintain a high standard of customer service. Each customer service representative is trained to communicate clearly and empathetically via email or chat, ensuring that customers receive timely and precise assistance. This focus on quality communication contributes significantly to Amazon's reputation for excellent customer service.

The impact of these practices is profound. The focus on clear, narrative communication fosters a culture of transparency and accountability. It also streamlines operations, as employees worldwide can access comprehensive records and insights, facilitating more efficient and informed work processes.

Amazon's emphasis on written communication has contributed to its operational efficiency and has maintained its innovative edge. By ensuring that ideas are communicated clearly and thoroughly, Amazon fosters an environment where creativity and practicality meet, driving continuous improvement and growth.

Amazon's effective use of written communication is a cornerstone of its remarkable success. By embedding this practice into its corporate culture, Amazon has created a dynamic and cohesive organization that continues to lead and innovate in multiple industries.

**How to improve written Communication Skills in the workplace?**

| Understand your audience | Be clear | Use structured formats | Stay updated with technology | Be consistent |

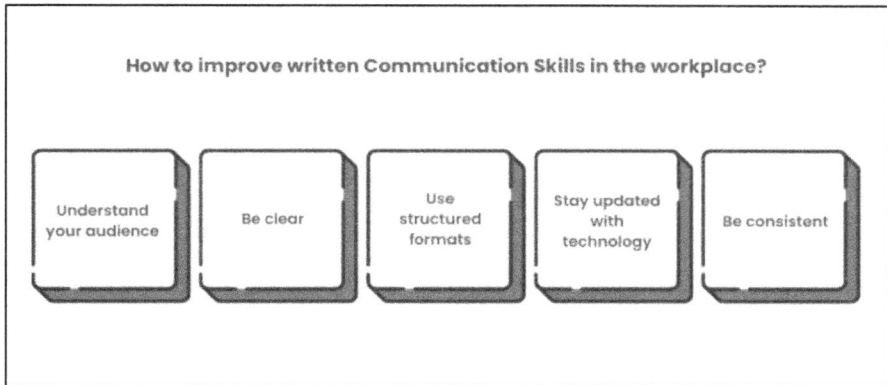

## Document Everything

An operations manual is a prime example of effective written communication. It is highly beneficial for communicating effectively in writing and establishing a clear process. By documenting all systems and operations in a clear format, you provide a comprehensive guide that ensures consistency and efficiency across the organization. This approach is a central knowledge repository detailing step-by-step procedures, roles, and responsibilities.

An operations manual is crucial because it standardizes processes, reduces uncertainty, and minimizes errors. It is a valuable resource for onboarding and training new employees, enabling them to understand and adapt to company procedures. Moreover, it helps maintain quality standards by providing clear instructions, thereby minimizing variations in execution and performance.

An operations manual supports continuous improvement by offering a reference point for evaluating and refining processes. It's a living document that can evolve with the business, incorporating feedback and new practices to enhance operational effectiveness. Overall, having all systems and operations documented in an operations manual fosters a culture of transparency and accountability, driving business growth and success.

**PROTIP:** Process documentation - When I go into a business to help them grow and succeed, I ask if they have an operations manual. If they don't have one, we help them create one. The business owners and leaders are excited when we start this project. Over the years, I've frequently encountered situations where departing team members take crucial information, such as passwords and usernames, for their tasks. Creating a manual outlining all the information needed for each operation will help a business run more smoothly.

Emails are a key form of written communication in the workplace, offering a time-stamped record of conversations that help keep track of discussions and decisions. They enable quick and efficient communication, allowing team members to share information easily and stay updated on important matters. This method not only ensures clarity in conveying messages but also serves as a reliable tool for documentation, making it easier to refer back to previous exchanges when needed.

Also, email communication is a huge time saver that can quickly solve issues and answer questions. This reduces staff fatigue and enhances engagement. Using email effectively enhances organization and supports seamless collaboration. Companies increasingly utilize interoffice communication systems. Amazon is a prime example of a company that has mastered the art of written communication, leveraging it to drive success across its global operations.

Different businesses have various business management systems. Every industry has its own options. We have implemented and trained teams on various systems to minimize confusion and enhance productivity. We encourage them to use the system with messaging and task management features that allow office staff to communicate efficiently. Emphasizing written communication in the workplace is crucial as it enhances both team and leadership dynamics.

By implementing effective written communication strategies, operations are more streamlined, customer care is coordinated efficiently, and daily tasks are managed more effectively. Introducing written communication practices boosts productivity and ensures that the team feels heard and engaged, ultimately leading to improved leadership skills as leaders become more proficient in their roles.

The greatest achievement is enhancing team security and fostering a more positive culture so the business soars!

**Practical Tips for Improving Written Communication in the Workplace:**

*1. Think First, Write Second:* Before you start typing, take a moment to think. Just like when you learned to write essays in school, it's important to outline your thoughts. Consider your purpose and key message. What do you want your audience to take away? This ensures your writing is focused and intentional.

**2. Be Straightforward:** Workplace communication is not the place for creative writing or long-winded explanations. People are pressed for time, so get to the point quickly. Put your main points at the top of the document, and be concise. A pro tip: if you're in a long email chain, change the subject line to reflect the latest topic so the conversation stays clear and relevant.

**3. Trim It Down:** Don't use five words when two will do. After writing, go back and see how you can tighten it up. Use contractions, cut unnecessary words, and replace complex terms with simpler ones. As MIT's Kara Blackburn suggests, use action verbs and keep your sentences direct.[45]

**4. Re-Read Before Sending:** Always re-read your writing before sending it out. Ask yourself if it's clear, well-structured, and easy to follow. Imagine you're the reader with no prior context—does it make sense? Reading it out loud can help you catch errors in punctuation or clarity. Tools like Grammarly can also help catch mistakes and improve readability.

**5. Practice Makes Progress:** Becoming a better writer takes time and practice. Don't be afraid to ask for feedback; remember that seeking help is okay before sending an important message. We're all working to improve, and collaboration can elevate the quality of communication.

**6. Know Your Audience:** Consider who you're writing to. If your audience prefers concise communication, tailor your message to be brief and to the point. Understanding their personality and communication styles will help you get a better response.

**7. Avoid Over-Communication:** Ask yourself, "Is this email necessary?" before sending it. Avoid adding unnecessary information, and always remain professional. Sarcasm or ambiguous language can easily be misinterpreted, so be clear and straightforward.

**8. Include a Call to Action:** If you want a response, include a clear call to action. This tells the recipient exactly what you're looking for, whether it's feedback, a decision, or further discussion.

**9. Save Your Best Work:** If you've written a particularly effective document or email, save it as a template. You can modify it for future use, saving time and ensuring you consistently deliver strong communication.

*10. Be Responsive.* For example, when someone sends a request via email or Slack, instead of waiting until you have a complete answer to respond, simply acknowledging the message goes a long way. A quick "I've got it, I'm working on it" keeps communication flowing. This is a great tip for being a proactive communicator. You can say, "Thanks for your message. I'll get back to you within 24 or 48 hours," or whatever time frame works for you. Then, it's crucial to follow through on what you promise. And if you're unable to meet that timeline, send a brief update, like "Hey, just keeping you in the loop—it's taking me longer than expected," or "I need more resources." This way, you're actively managing the relationship and communication, preventing the other person from feeling left in the dark.

**PROTIP:** Use a "PS or PostScript" - Use a "PS" at the end of your email. It's a powerful tool, whether you're sending something physically or digitally. Think about when you receive a message with a "PS"—your eye goes right there! If you're dealing with someone who's not a great communicator, and you want to keep the door open for follow-up without it feeling awkward, you can add a line like, "PS: As a courtesy, if I haven't heard back from you in twenty-four hours, I'll follow up." This gives you the freedom to reach out again without feeling uncomfortable.

Following these tips can improve your written communication, making your messages more effective and professional while fostering better workplace productivity.

## Importance of Non-Verbal Communication

Last week, I had the opportunity to present at a webinar that attracted 3,400 sign-ups. To our surprise, 15,108 people showed up! As we were setting up, I had a conversation with the facilitator. A few things caught me off guard. I asked, "Are everyone's cameras going to be on?" I understood they'd be muted to avoid background noise, but I hoped to see people's faces. The facilitator replied, "No, we turn all the cameras off," and explained it was due to bandwidth issues, especially for attendees in other countries. Still, this left me uneasy.

As a presenter, I rely heavily on nonverbal feedback—body language, facial expressions—to gauge how my message is landing. I like to know if people are engaged, nodding, or seeming confused so that I can adjust on the fly. When I learned their cameras would be off, I realized I wouldn't have that immediate feedback loop.

But what surprised me was that the facilitator also mentioned they usually keep *my* camera off. "No way," I thought. "If I'm presenting, people need to see me!"

The outcome was super positive. After the webinar, I received numerous emails from attendees praising my presentation. They enjoyed the information and loved my animated and passionate delivery style. They found the course not only informative but also engaging and entertaining. This experience reinforced that effective communication extends beyond words; it involves our **facial expressions, gestures, and overall presence.** Visual cues like leaning in as an active listener can significantly enhance the connection between the speaker and the audience. This two-way verbal and non-verbal communication exchange leads to better understanding and collaboration, ultimately leading to more successful interactions and outcomes.

In another instance, I noticed a colleague's need for more engagement during a conversation. Her slumped shoulders and disengaged expression indicated a disconnect from the discussion. Recognizing these cues allowed me to address the issue directly. I invited her to share her perspective, ensuring she felt heard. This experience highlighted the value of cultivating awareness and emotional intelligence in communication. We can be more adept communicators by being present and tuning in to various non-verbal signals, such as eye movement, body posture, and vocal changes. This attentiveness helps us interpret underlying messages and builds a more authentic and empathetic dialogue.

Communication isn't just about your words; your facial expressions, hand gestures, and body language speak loud and clear to anyone paying attention. Your passion doesn't only come through your voice; it's in how you move and the energy you exude. Thankfully, they let me keep my camera on for the webinar. The feedback I received was incredibly positive. People appreciated how animated and engaging I was—not just what I said but how I expressed it.

## It's Holistic

This experience highlighted something: communication isn't just verbal; it's holistic. It's about using your hands and expressions and even leaning into a conversation. All these non-verbal cues enhance the connection between speaker and listener, creating a dynamic feedback loop beyond words.

When I present, I'm constantly reading the room for signs that people are receiving what I'm saying. I recall a company I worked with where I could tell immediately if one of the team members wasn't connecting with me simply by watching her body language. I knew to check in if I saw her slumping or her face losing focus. Maybe she's interpreting my message differently, or perhaps she's disengaged. Either way, the body always tells the truth, even when the person doesn't speak up.

Awareness is a key to nonverbal communication. You need to be present and attuned to the countless nonverbal signals people send. They can be in their eyes, their posture, the distance they maintain, or even a change in their tone. Picking up on these cues allows for better communication and connection.

Another time, during a recent speaking engagement, I emphasized the importance of having the right people in the right seats within an organization, drawing an analogy where everyone on a bus faces forward. To drive this point home, I used my body language to physically demonstrate the concept, recognizing that my spoken words alone might not fully convey the message's impact. Combining verbal articulation and physical demonstration created a more compelling and memorable experience. We constantly communicate non-verbally, and our body language can often speak volumes beyond our words.

Non-verbal communication is a fundamental aspect of human interaction. It complements verbal communication, often conveying messages more powerfully than words alone. Mastering this skill is crucial because it encompasses a wide range of expressions, including body language, facial expressions, and gestures, which can significantly impact the clarity and effectiveness of the communication process.

A leader who maintains eye contact and uses open gestures can reinforce their sincerity and build trust among team members. Conversely, crossed arms or averted eyes might unintentionally signal disinterest or defensiveness, undermining the spoken message. Understanding and controlling non-verbal expressions is essential to ensure that communication is perceived as intended and does not result in misunderstandings or negative outcomes.

Leaders and team members who actively hone their non-verbal communication skills can significantly enhance their ability to express themselves and support one another. They can create a more supportive and cohesive team environment by being mindful of their and others' body language and cues. Non-verbal communication is especially effective in expressing empathy and understanding, which are crucial for teamwork and collaboration.

For example, nodding in agreement or leaning forward during discussions can demonstrate engagement and encouragement, encouraging a more open and communicative atmosphere. This form of communication can bridge gaps and convey messages that words may fail to express. It's an invaluable tool in professional settings.

I also have learned that non-verbal communication is vital in ensuring that messages are conveyed and received. I always advise my teams to maintain eye contact when interacting with customers and colleagues. By sitting eye to eye, knee to knee, and heart to heart, we create a balanced and equal atmosphere that helps prevent feelings of intimidation or miscommunication. This approach is especially important for taller individuals, like my six-foot-four son, whose height can unintentionally come across as domineering. Sitting down during conversations makes our messages more likely to be well-received, fostering open and understanding dialogues. This approach applies to people who are smaller in stature as well.

Reflecting on my journey, I've realized the importance of being conscious of my nonverbal cues, regardless of my size. Despite being five feet six inches, I've learned to manage the energy I project through my body language, tone, and eye contact.

# Culture Matters in Communication

Understanding cultural backgrounds is crucial if you want to interpret non-verbal signals accurately. For example, a colleague of mine refrains from making eye contact with male authority figures. In his culture, looking at an authority figure is considered disrespectful. This reminds me to avoid assumptions about trustworthiness based solely on eye contact. This cultural awareness enriches communication by fostering respect for diverse backgrounds and customs.

## A New Era - Zoom Communication

Enter the "Zoom Era"! How we now conduct our meetings on Zoom comes with a whole new set of etiquette rules. I've found that I need to adapt my nonverbal communication to this new environment. Have you?

These adaptations help mimic the connection and attentiveness found in face-to-face meetings. My insights on Zoom etiquette, such as avoiding multitasking and staying focused, highlight the importance of deliberate effort in virtual interactions. The evolving nature of non-verbal communication requires continuous adaptation and awareness to connect with others, whether in person or online.

The interplay between verbal and non-verbal communication is dynamic. Each can enhance or contradict the other. When they align, they create a powerful synergy that enhances the message. However, a mismatch, such as saying "I'm listening" while glancing at a phone, can create confusion and distrust. Monitoring non-verbal cues ensures consistency between what is said and what is shown. This consistency not only aids in conveying messages more effectively but also strengthens relationships and collaboration. By mastering non-verbal communication, leaders and team members can facilitate clearer, more productive interactions, ultimately leading to more successful outcomes.

# Visual Communication

Visual communication involves strategically using visual elements—such as images, videos, and graphs—to convey information or ideas effectively and engagingly. Visual communication can also correlate to what your company is communicating by its visual appeal.

In our fast-paced, digital world, communicating visually is crucial for organizations and individuals. This form of communication enhances branding efforts and facilitates interpersonal communication within teams by making complex information more accessible.

## The Importance of Visual Communication

Visual communication is vital. It's a highly efficient information-sharing medium that provides a consistent experience and significantly enhances information retention rates.

Studies show that the brain processes images and videos up to 60,000 times faster than text, making visual communication incredibly effective. [46] People retain 80% of what they see, compared to just 20% of what they read or hear. This makes integrating visual elements into communication strategies essential. It aligns with most individuals' natural processing capabilities, ensuring messages are clear and impactful.

Visual communication is invaluable for dental practices, especially in multidisciplinary treatment planning. Visual aids illustrate treatment plans, helping patients understand the sequence and scope of complex procedures.

This visual clarity fosters trust and reduces anxiety, offering patients a transparent view of their healthcare journey.

Visual communication is key to moving a customer down the sales funnel. Tools for effective visual communication can include a customer journey map that shows your company's "way." The idea that a picture is worth a thousand words is very accurate.

When explaining important information to customers, visuals can help them understand more complex concepts. Long blocks of text can be overwhelming, so rather than utilizing this, consider using charts, graphs, or diagrams to visually show data and main ideas.

## Facilitate Collaboration and Decision-Making

Visual communication benefits external audiences and is a powerful tool for internal collaboration. Whiteboards, diagrams, and flowcharts can simplify brainstorming and problem-solving sessions. Project management tools with visual maps, like Asana or Gantt charts, help teams map out workflows, track progress, and make decisions more efficiently.

By visualizing ideas and processes, teams can identify bottlenecks, spot opportunities for improvement, and communicate more clearly. This leads to faster, more informed decision-making and ensures everyone is on the same page.

## Visual Communication in Virtual Settings

The shift to virtual platforms like Zoom highlights the importance of visual communication in maintaining engagement.

Effective visual setups—including proper lighting, uncluttered backgrounds, and intentional eye contact—ensure clarity and connection in digital spaces. This transition requires new etiquette and skills. Visual communication is as crucial online as in person. We maintain eye contact through the camera and use appropriate lighting and backdrop settings.

**PROTIP**: When on Zoom, use a high-resolution camera and three-point lighting (position lights in three ways) to help make your nonverbal communication and presence POP.

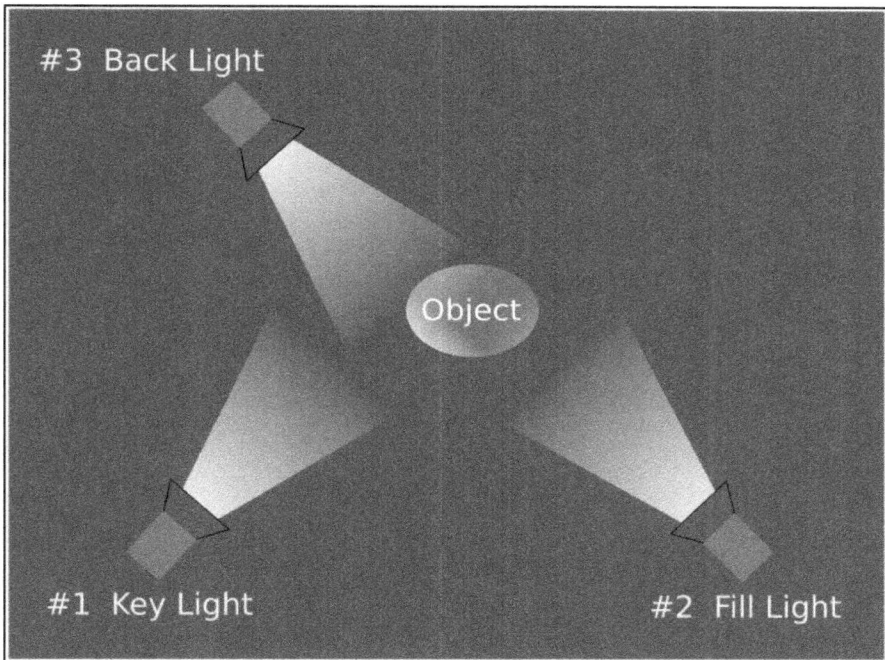

## Psychological and Practical Benefits

Consistent visual branding creates psychological safety. It provides a cohesive and familiar experience for employees and customers. This consistency reduces stress and enhances trust. Individuals are more likely to engage with uniformly presented and reliable information. Tools like company event flyers and culture handbooks enriched with images and infographics streamline communication and create an engaging, inclusive environment.

Visual elements mitigate the effects of information overload, a common challenge in today's workplaces. You can make your messages more digestible and engaging by reducing reliance on lengthy text using images, GIFs, and videos. This approach fosters higher engagement and ensures that communication is meaningful and memorable.

### The Science Behind Visual Processing

The brain's visual cortex is significantly larger than the area responsible for reading words (Broca's area). This is why visual presentations communicate complex information so effectively. Visual content engages more of the brain's capacity, improving retention and understanding, making it a superior method for conveying information.

Visual communication is vital to modern interaction, enhancing understanding and connection across various contexts. By embracing its potential, organizations can improve internal dynamics and strengthen external relationships, paving the way for success in an increasingly visual world.

### Building Emotional Connections

Visuals can evoke emotions in ways that text alone cannot. Think about the impact of a compelling brand story video or an image that reflects a company's mission. By incorporating colors, imagery, and design, you can connect emotionally with your employees, clients, or stakeholders.

Companies that use visuals to tell stories about their values, products, or success stories can build stronger, more personal connections with their customers. These connections improve trust and loyalty, which are critical for long-term business relationships.

**Strengthening Branding and Consistency**

Consistent visual communication is key to building and reinforcing a strong brand identity. Logos, color schemes, typography, and overall design aesthetics affect how a company is perceived. Consistency in these visual elements across all business materials—from emails to presentations to social media—reinforces brand recognition and credibility.

A strong visual identity also ensures that your message is clear and coherent, no matter the medium. By maintaining consistency, your audience will immediately recognize your brand and the professionalism that comes with it.

# SECTION IV
## LEADERSHIP

# LEADERSHIP

Leadership is the art of motivating and guiding individuals or groups toward achieving a common goal, often by inspiring confidence and fostering teamwork. It involves setting a vision, making strategic decisions, and empowering others to realize their potential.

A great leader, on the other hand, is someone who not only possesses leadership skills but also demonstrates integrity, empathy, and the ability to inspire others. They lead by example, communicate effectively, and create an environment where innovation and collaboration flourish. So, what does being a great leader mean?

We've all experienced the difference between a great boss and a not-so-great boss. In my early twenties, I began a journey that would forever shape my understanding of leadership. I worked for US Marketing and Promotions, a company based in Marina Del Rey, California, while living in the bustling energy of New York City. My task was daunting yet exciting—overseeing the Anheuser Busch Making Friends Program.

This involved hiring and training brand ambassadors across eight different markets. I was managing up to two hundred staff members at any given time. It was challenging, but I was fortunate to have Jennifer Houston as my boss. Jen was the epitome of a true leader. She led with collaboration and support, much like a coach, nurturing each team member's strengths. Her ability to provide praise when earned and constructive feedback when needed taught me that real leadership isn't about being liked but guiding others through growth and challenges.

Before Jen, my leadership experience was quite different under a boss I'll call Peter Smith. Peter was brilliant and filled with visionary ideas. His style was authoritarian, grounded in control and demands. Working under him was intimidating, and his management approach often unnerved me. I appreciated his attention to detail, but his strictness made the work environment tense and unenjoyable. In stark contrast, Jen's supportive nature felt like having a parent figure who balanced praise with constructive boundaries. Her style created an environment where I felt encouraged and motivated to excel.

These contrasting experiences taught me valuable lessons about the kind of leader I wanted to be. As a young leader, I faced skepticism due to my age, especially when leading older, more experienced team members. However, my passion for the company and dedication to supporting my team propelled me. I sought advice and continued learning to enhance my skills. I was always aiming for personal and professional growth. Jen's example showed me the power of a collaborative and supportive approach.

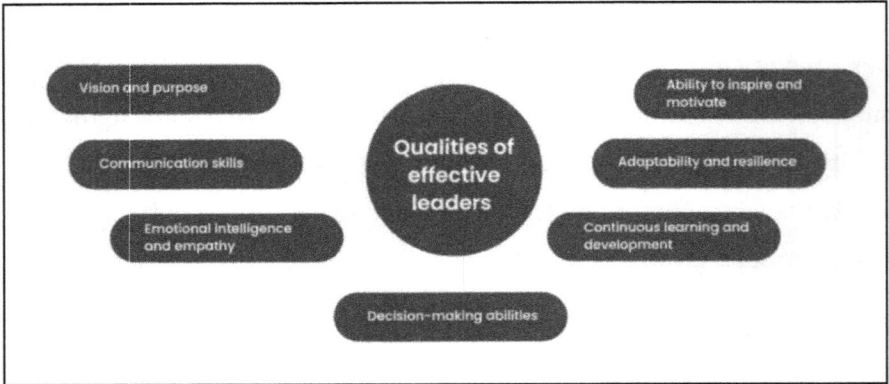

I learned that leadership is about authenticity and continuous learning. Initially, I felt the need to "fake it till I made it," but as time went on, authenticity became crucial. It's a journey of self-discovery where the goal is to model the behavior you wish to see in others. By sharing knowledge and encouraging others, we also uplift them into leadership roles. This ongoing growth journey is essential for us and those we lead, ensuring we all thrive and succeed together. My experiences taught me that positive leadership and a commitment to continuous learning are key to creating thriving, supportive work environments.

As leaders, we often assume multiple roles, each essential in driving our teams toward success. One role is a motivator, where we lead through encouragement, fostering an environment that empowers individuals to perform at their best. This involves recognizing individual and team accomplishments, boosting morale, and cultivating a positive atmosphere that enhances productivity and innovation. Providing this support inspires our teams to reach their full potential.

Beyond being the motivator, leaders also step into mentor, strategist, and mediator roles. As mentors, we provide guidance and support, sharing our knowledge and experience to help team members grow and succeed. As strategists, we are responsible for setting the vision, navigating the path forward, and making decisions that align with our goals and values. When conflicts or challenges arise, we must become well-trained mediators, facilitating open communication and understanding to resolve issues and maintain harmony within the team.

Switching seamlessly between these roles requires adaptability and a deep understanding of each team member's needs and strengths. By embracing these diverse roles, leaders can cultivate a cohesive and resilient team capable of achieving great things together. This multifaceted approach strengthens the team and reinforces the leader's capacity to inspire and drive lasting success.

# The Story Of Dr. Sarah - A Client Who Learned to Step Up

Dr. Sarah had always seen herself as the cheerleader of her chiropractic clinic, rallying her team and celebrating their successes. But she quickly learned that being a business owner meant stepping into roles far beyond cheerleading. One day, she had to wear a different hat—that of a mediator.

Two of her most trusted staff members, Lisa and Mark, had been at odds for weeks. Tensions had started over a scheduling mix-up but had become more personal. The once harmonious clinic felt frustrated. Sarah knew she had to step in.

As the clinic leader, Sarah understood her responsibility wasn't just to manage the day-to-day operations but to guide her team through challenges, personal or professional. She had seen conflict before but was still learning to navigate these rough waters. In her early leadership days, she operated more as a manager—focused on tasks and goals. She didn't have the skills to mediate conflicts like this, but she knew she had to step up.

She called Lisa and Mark into her office for a private meeting. Sitting them down, Sarah reminded them of the clinic's vision—a place of healing and collaboration. "Beyond being a cheerleader," she began, *"I see myself as a mentor, strategist, and mediator. Right now, I'm here to mediate. We're all on the same team, and I know we can find a way to communicate openly and with understanding."*

At first, both employees were hesitant, their arms crossed and eyes avoiding one another. But Sarah had learned that effective mediation wasn't about picking sides. It was about promoting communication and guiding them toward understanding. She encouraged them to express their perspectives without interruption, emphasizing the need for honesty and respect.

As each spoke, the tension started to lift. What seemed like a deep conflict was merely a series of misunderstandings and unspoken frustrations. Lisa admitted that the scheduling mistake had made her feel undervalued. Mark shared that he had been overwhelmed with his workload, which led to his snapping in frustration.

As the strategist, Sarah helped them see how their needs could be addressed while aligning with the clinic's values. Together, they brainstormed ways to improve communication and reduce scheduling errors in the future, creating a clear path forward. By the end of the meeting, the atmosphere had shifted. There were no dramatic apologies, but there was something better—mutual understanding and a willingness to work together again.

As she watched them leave the office, Sarah felt accomplished. She had seamlessly switched between her roles—mentor, strategist, and mediator—

and, in doing so, had cultivated the environment she had always envisioned for her clinic. Leadership wasn't just about being a cheerleader. It was about guiding the team through the storms and becoming stronger on the other side.

For Sarah, this was another step in her evolution from manager to true leader who could adapt to her team's needs and inspire lasting success.

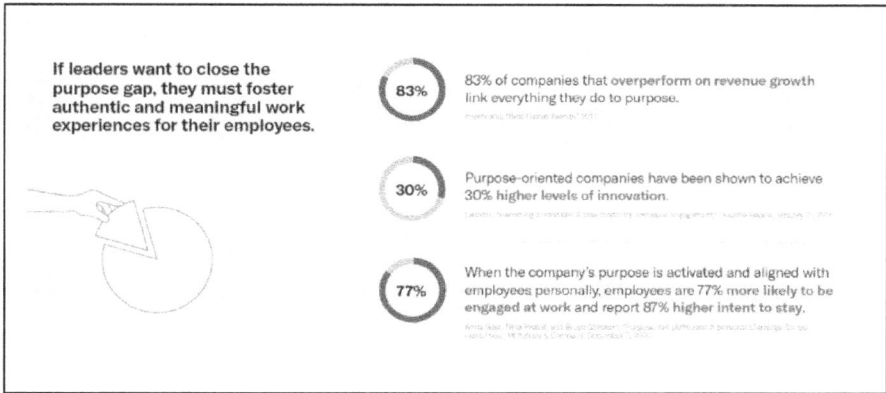

**If leaders want to close the purpose gap, they must foster authentic and meaningful work experiences for their employees.**

**83%** 83% of companies that overperform on revenue growth link everything they do to purpose.

**30%** Purpose-oriented companies have been shown to achieve 30% higher levels of innovation.

**77%** When the company's purpose is activated and aligned with employees personally, employees are 77% more likely to be engaged at work and report 87% higher intent to stay.

# What is Authentic Leadership?

A true leader leads by example, fostering strong relationships with individuals and teams alike. They ensure that all reach their full potential and simultaneously work to achieve traction in meeting organizational goals.

There is a significant distinction between being a leader and being a *true leader*. While individuals may often speak about leadership, they do not embody the qualities of a true leader. The influence of a true leader resonates in every aspect of an organization. It's essential to understand the traits that define authentic leadership.

Authentic leadership is characterized by individuals who demonstrate integrity, accountability, and a **commitment to making moral decisions rather than pursuing short-term gains**. Guided by their core values, authentic leaders align their actions with those principles, earning the trust of employees, peers, and stakeholders. This approach nurtures a transparent and approachable work environment, enhancing team performance.

What sets authentic leadership apart is the leader's motivation. Authentic leaders aim to build meaningful relationships with their teams, working collaboratively toward goals aligned with the organization's mission and purpose—not merely focusing on financial outcomes.

According to a study in the Leadership and Organization Development Journal,[47] "employees' perception of authentic leadership serves as the strongest predictor of job satisfaction and positively impacts work-related attitudes and happiness."

In addition, research detailed in the Harvard Business Review[48] shows that a majority of employees believe authenticity in the workplace leads to benefits such as:

- Better relationships with colleagues
- Higher levels of trust
- Greater productivity
- A more positive working environment

For leaders who want to take their business to the next level, investing time in developing their authentic leadership skills can be incredibly valuable. What characterizes authentic leadership, and why is it a worthy pursuit? Here are five traits of authentic leaders offered by Harvard Business School Professor Nancy Koehn:

**Characteristics of Authentic Leaders**

1. They're Committed to Bettering Themselves
2. They Cultivate Self-Awareness
3. They're Disciplined
4. They're Mission-Driven
5. They Inspire Faith

Harvard Business School Online

## 1. Committed to Bettering Themselves

Authentic leaders "walk the walk" instead of just "talking the talk." They are on a path to continuous growth and are committed to bettering themselves. For example, they regularly enroll in courses to improve their skills.

## 2. They Cultivate Self-Awareness

When leaders are more self-aware, profitability soars. A high level of self-awareness contributes to career success and effective leadership. New research from the Korn Ferry Institute shows that it correlates with corporate performance. Using Korn Ferry's ProSpective Assessment, we examined 6,977 self-assessments to identify "blind spots" in individuals' leadership characteristics and compared these results against the financial data of 486 publicly traded companies.

The analysis revealed companies with a higher rate of return (ROR) also employ professionals who exhibit higher levels of self-awareness. Stock performance was tracked over thirty months, during which the companies with more self-aware employees consistently outperformed the rest. Despite its close association with high performance, self-awareness is generally in short supply, but can be developed in leaders." [35]

## 3. They're Disciplined

Authentic leadership goes beyond developing self-awareness; it requires consistently putting it into practice, which demands discipline. Regularly check in with yourself during daily activities—such as providing feedback or interacting with colleagues—to ensure self-awareness guides your actions.

By better understanding your motivations and limitations, you can better define your leadership style and create a professional development plan that leverages your strengths while addressing areas for improvement.

## 4. They're Mission-Driven

A strong commitment to a clear mission is essential for authentic leadership and business success. A shared sense of purpose boosts employee engagement and enhances the success of transformational initiatives.

## 5. They Inspire Faith

Earning colleagues' trust and inspiring them to rally around a shared mission is fundamental to effective leadership. We need to empower our teams to have the courage to take a leap of faith when the going gets tough. You must help your team believe the mission is worth pursuing, even when facing obstacles.

When communicating organizational changes or evaluating the challenges of scaling a business, be transparent with your team and connect with their core motivations.

# Stepping Up

Recognizing who within your organization has the potential to step into this role—and who may not be the right fit—is crucial. Identifying the qualities of a true leader is vital for organizational success.

Being a true leader means having emotional intelligence, communicating well, and holding yourself accountable. It's about lifting others and valuing them. You need courage and a clear vision. Early in my career, even though I was in leadership roles, I didn't always feel like a true leader. I remember working at an advertising agency when I was eighteen years old. I was leading teams but lacked self-awareness. I could communicate, but I still needed to improve at it.

The best leaders aren't born; they're made. Anyone can become a leader if they're willing to be self-aware, grow, and be vulnerable, with healthy boundaries. A manager focuses on managing teams and getting daily tasks done, while a leader looks ahead, thinks innovatively, and sees the bigger picture beyond just operations. Leaders cast a vision for others to follow.

I was young and eager to learn when I first started managing practices. I quickly realized that great leadership develops over time. While we might have traits that guide us toward leadership, we must learn the skills. I've grown by watching and learning from other great leaders. Over the years, I've picked up a few crucial lessons. One of the most important is the need to communicate clearly.

It's about understanding who you're talking to and adapting your communication style to fit them. Great leaders know how to do this to ensure their team members receive information in a way that leads to positive outcomes.

Being passionate about our work is another key element, even if it means our ideas are sometimes unconventional. It's fine to be a bit unpopular if it leads to innovation and success. I believe in a collaborative leadership style where we welcome new ideas and opinions from the team. It's not about having things my way but about listening to everyone and finding the best path forward. I genuinely feel like I work for my team, not vice versa. It's my mission to help them thrive and perform their jobs efficiently. Supporting a thriving environment is essential, and I strive to lift my team, offering praise and encouragement whenever I can.

Building strong relationships is crucial, too. Great leaders are not threatened by others; they encourage and support them. I focus on creating good connections and fostering mutually beneficial relationships. This approach helps build trust and promote positive outcomes. Leading by example is vital; it's not just about giving orders but showing how things are done. When we do this well, it builds trust within the team and enhances our collective success.

Lastly, great leaders never stop learning. I am constantly seeking to grow both professionally and personally. Whether reading a new book or learning from other leaders with different perspectives, I always seek to expand my knowledge. This ongoing learning benefits me and the team as I bring back new insights that help us all thrive. This continuous journey of growth and development makes leadership truly effective.

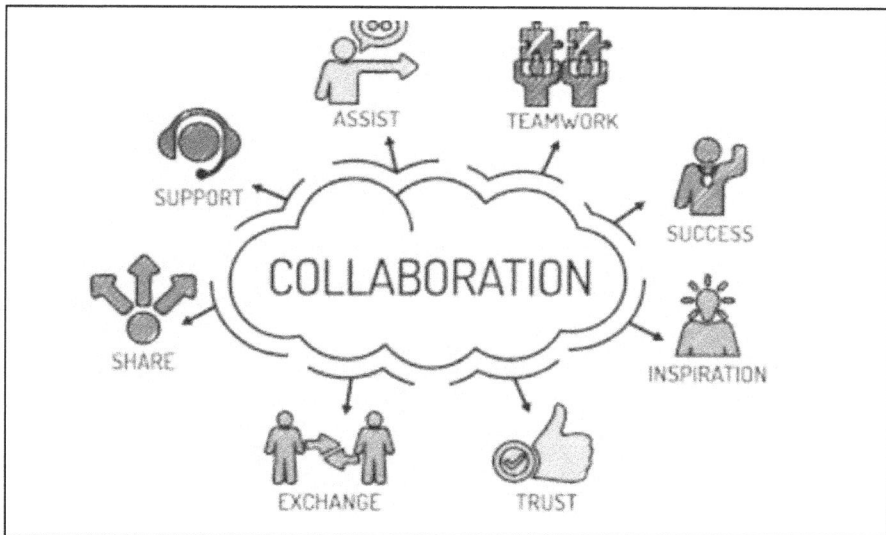

## Leader vs. Manager

About ten years ago, I started coaching Mark, a manager for a client's small family-run business. Mark was known for getting things done efficiently, but he lacked a deeper connection with his team. He had been with the company for about five years when he approached the owner after an incident with a team member. This incident made him aware that his approach was creating a culture of compliance, not commitment.

Working together, I helped him begin his transformation with self-awareness. Through the process, Mark recognized that his focus on tasks, rather than people, was holding the team back. After a few months of working together, he embraced authenticity. He started sharing more about himself with his employees and creating a space where they felt comfortable doing the same. As he grew, he prioritized integrity, ensuring his words and actions aligned, which built trust within the team.

Within the framework of our coaching relationship, Mark developed critical thinking as a cornerstone of his leadership. Instead of making quick decisions based on immediate needs, he began to analyze challenges from multiple perspectives, involving his team in the process. Mark also learned to adapt, shifting strategies as the business environment changed, which made the team more resilient.

Looking back, I can see how negotiation became one of his key skills. When disputes arose or resources were limited, Mark sought win-win solutions. He relied on empathy and fairness to resolve conflicts. He learned to motivate his team not through directives but by inspiring them with a clear vision for the company's future and encouraging them to grow within their roles. He did this through weekly meetings with a specific time for team members to speak their truth and share their challenges.

*Team building was where Mark truly shined. He stopped seeing himself as the one with all the answers and began cultivating a culture where collaboration was valued.*

Mark made thoughtful, inclusive decisions, empowering others to contribute to the company's success. His influence grew as he communicated openly and consistently, ensuring everyone understood the company's goals and their role in achieving them.

Mark's evolution from manager to leader was a journey of growth, marked by a deep commitment to personal development and his team's success. What had once been a job of managing tasks became a passion for leading people, and the small business thrived.

# Leadership Styles - What Kind of Leader Are You?

*"Being a great leader means recognizing that different circumstances may call for different approaches, "* - **Daniel Goleman**

## Emotional Intelligence

The four domains of EI as described by Daniel Goleman

### RECOGNITION

#### SELF-AWARENESS
(PERSONAL COMPETENCE)

- Awareness of your moods and emotional state
- Interpreting your actions, feelings, and thoughts objectively
- Recognizing how your behavior impacts others
- Paying attention to how others influenced your emotional state

### REGULATION

#### SELF-MANAGEMENT
(PERSONAL COMPETENCE)

- Self-control + ability to redirect disruptive impulses
- Adaptability / handling change
- Initiative and optimism
- Handling conflict effectively
- Pursuing goals despite setbacks
- Acting in alignment with your values

#### SOCIAL-AWARENESS
(SOCIAL COMPETENCE)

- Picking up on the mood in the room
- Caring what others are going through
- Hearing what the other person is 'really' saying
- Finding common ground and building rapport

#### RELATIONSHIP-MANAGEMENT
(SOCIAL COMPETENCE)

- Managing conflict effectively
- Teamwork and collaboration - getting along well with others
- Communication - clearly expressing ideas/information
- Having empathy - using sensitivity to anothers feelings to manage interactions successfully
- Developing others, inspirational leadership

LEAD GRIT

Leadership styles are as diverse as those who embody them, each bringing unique strengths and challenges. Visit www.CultureCatalystBook.com/quizzes and take our leadership quiz. We invite you to embark on a journey of self-reflection to understand your approach to leadership better. Whether you lead with a collaborative spirit, a commanding presence, or somewhere in between, your style profoundly impacts your team's dynamics and the overall success of your organization.

By examining your leadership approach, you enhance your effectiveness and foster stronger, more meaningful relationships with those you lead. Discovering and embracing your leadership style is a crucial step in your journey to becoming the best leader you can be.

Drawing on research and experience, Goleman identified six distinct leadership styles that managers can adapt depending on their team members' situations and needs. He first introduced these styles in his 2000 Harvard Business Review article, "Leadership That Gets Results,"[37,] and they have since been widely recognized as an essential framework for effective leadership. The six leadership styles are:

- Coercive leadership entails demanding immediate compliance.
- Authoritative leadership is about mobilizing people toward a vision.
- Affiliative leadership centers around building emotional bonds.
- Democratic leadership involves creating consensus.
- Pacesetting leadership involves expecting excellence and self-direction.
- Coaching leadership focuses on developing people for the future.

So, which of these leadership styles is best? Well, the answer might surprise you. According to the Harvard Business Review,[49] research conducted by the consulting firm Hay/McBer, which draws on a random sample of 3,871 executives selected from a database of more than 20,000 executives worldwide, takes much of the mystery out of effective leadership. The research indicates that leaders with the best results **rely on more than just a single leadership style; they use most of them seamlessly and in different measures to fit the business situation**.

What's surprising about this research is its implications for action. It offers a tuned-in understanding of how leadership styles affect performance and results and clear guidance on when a leader should switch between them.

*Most importantly, the research finds that each leadership style springs from different components of emotional intelligence!*

### The Six Leadership Styles at a Glance

Our research found that leaders use six styles, each springing from different components of emotional intelligence. Here is a summary of the styles, their origin, when they work best, and their impact on an organization's climate and thus its performance.

|  | | Coercive | Authoritative |
|---|---|---|---|
| The leader's modus operandi | | Demands immediate compliance | Mobilizes people toward a vision |
| The style in a phrase | | "Do what I tell you." | "Come with me." |
| Underlying emotional intelligence competencies | | Drive to achieve, initiative, self-control | Self-confidence, empathy, change catalyst |
| When the style works best | | In a crisis, to kick start a turnaround, or with problem employees | When changes require a new vision, or when a clear direction is needed |
| Overall impact on climate | | Negative | Most strongly positive |

| Affiliative | Democratic | Pacesetting | Coaching |
|---|---|---|---|
| Creates harmony and builds emotional bonds | Forges consensus through participation | Sets high standards for performance | Develops people for the future |
| "People come first." | "What do you think?" | "Do as I do, now." | "Try this." |
| Empathy, building relationships, communication | Collaboration, team leadership, communication | Conscientiousness, drive to achieve, initiative | Developing others, empathy, self-awareness |
| To heal rifts in a team or to motivate people during stressful circumstances | To build buy-in or consensus, or to get input from valuable employees | To get quick results from a highly motivated and competent team | To help an employee improve performance or develop long-term strengths |
| Positive | Positive | Negative | Positive |

## Coercive Leadership

Coercive leadership is characterized by authority and pressure to achieve compliance and immediate results, often at the expense of employee morale. For example, in a manufacturing plant, the manager might implement a coercive leadership style by enforcing strict quotas and threatening disciplinary action for any team member who fails to meet targets.

This approach can create a high-pressure environment where employees feel compelled to work harder out of fear rather than motivation. While it may lead to short-term productivity gains, the long-term effects often include decreased job satisfaction, high turnover rates, and a lack of innovation, as employees may feel discouraged from voicing their ideas or concerns.

**Example:**

A well-known example of coercive leadership in business is Howard Schultz, the former CEO of Starbucks, during the company's rapid expansion phase in the early 2000s. While Schultz is often praised for his visionary leadership and emphasis on employee engagement, he faced significant challenges that led him to adopt a more coercive style, particularly during the economic downturn in 2008.

As the company struggled with declining sales and increased competition, Schultz implemented strict measures to stabilize the business. He set ambitious financial targets and pressured store managers to meet those goals. Schultz's coercive approach involved enforcing strict operational standards and closely monitoring performance metrics. For instance, he would often visit stores unannounced to assess adherence to these standards, creating an environment where managers felt compelled to achieve results or face potential consequences.

While this leadership style led to a short-term turnaround in Starbucks' performance, it also created tension within the workforce. Some employees felt demoralized by the pressure to meet high expectations, leading to decreased morale and job satisfaction. Recognizing the negative impact of this approach, Schultz later shifted back to a more participative leadership style, focused on employee training and engagement initiatives. This facilitated a culture that aligned more closely with the company's values.

This example illustrates how coercive leadership can effectively drive immediate results during crises, but it also highlights the potential downsides, including employee dissatisfaction and a lack of innovation. Schultz's experience reminds us that while coercive measures may yield short-term gains, sustainable success often requires a balance of different leadership styles that prioritize both results and the well-being of employees.

## Authoritative Style

Of the six leadership styles, the authoritative one is the most effective, driving up every aspect of "climate," or working atmosphere.

Leaders with an Authoritative style understand the importance of creating a clear vision; they are Visionaries. They help their teams understand how each individual contributes and how their work fits into the big picture. This helps team members understand what they do matters and how it matters.

*"Clear is kind, unclear is unkind."* - **Brene Brown**

The Authoritative style leader understands that clarity is the underpinning of success. Authoritative leaders see the big picture and work to get the team on board. An authoritative leader is characterized by a clear vision and a strong sense of direction. They effectively guide their team with confidence and empathy. They establish clear expectations and provide the necessary support to help team members achieve their goals while encouraging autonomy and creativity. Authoritative leaders foster an environment of trust and collaboration where employees feel valued and empowered to contribute.

This balances structure with flexibility, allowing for constructive feedback and open communication, ultimately driving individual and organizational success. By inspiring and motivating their teams, authoritative leaders cultivate a culture of engagement and accountability.

**Example:**

**Indra Nooyi,** the former CEO of PepsiCo, used the authoritative style to great effect. When Nooyi took over the company in 2006, she faced the challenge of revitalizing PepsiCo's brand and product line in a rapidly changing market increasingly focused on health and sustainability.

Nooyi adopted an authoritative leadership style. She brought a clear vision and strong commitment to strategic change. She articulated her goal of transforming PepsiCo into a "global leader in convenient foods and beverages while promoting sustainability." The "Performance with Purpose" vision aimed to balance financial performance with social and environmental responsibility.

To implement this vision, Nooyi engaged with her team and encouraged collaboration across different divisions. She was known for her open-door policy, making herself accessible to employees at all levels. By fostering a culture of trust and accountability, Nooyi empowered her managers to take ownership of their projects while aligning them with the company's overarching goals.

One of her significant initiatives was the introduction of healthier product options, responding to growing consumer demand for nutritious food and beverages. She led the effort to reformulate existing products and expand the company's portfolio to include healthier choices. This strategic shift required guidance from Nooyi and the involvement of various teams working together to develop and market these new products effectively.

Under Nooyi's leadership, PepsiCo saw substantial growth, impressive revenue increases, and a strengthened brand reputation. Her ability to set a clear vision, communicate effectively, and inspire her team while focusing on performance exemplifies the positive impact of the authoritative leadership style.

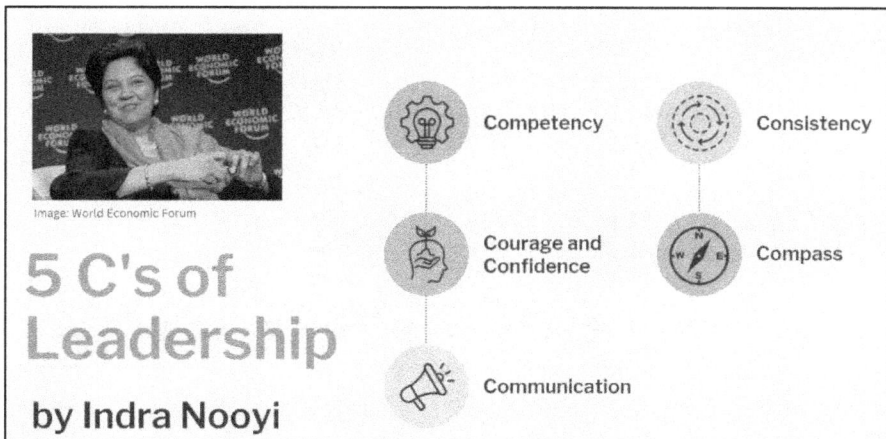

Image: World Economic Forum

5 C's of Leadership by Indra Nooyi

Competency

Consistency

Courage and Confidence

Compass

Communication

**When Authoritative Leadership Doesn't Work**

Authoritative leadership isn't a one-size-fits-all approach. This style may not fit an inexperienced leader working with a team of seasoned experts or peers. Their team may perceive them as arrogant or disconnected. Managers who become overly authoritative risk undermining the egalitarian spirit essential for a high-functioning team.

Egalitarian leadership means that the boss doesn't separate themselves from their subordinates; they are equal. A strong boss is necessary in hierarchical behavior; leaders must set themselves apart from their subordinates. Despite these limitations, leaders would be wise to embrace the authoritative style more frequently, as it often encourages clarity and motivation within the team.

## Getting Molecular: The Impact of Leadership Styles on Drivers of Climate

Our research investigated how each leadership style affected the six drivers of climate, or working atmosphere. The figures below show the correlation between each leadership style and each aspect of climate. So, for instance, if we look at the climate driver of flexibility, we see that the coercive style has a -.28 correlation while the democratic style has a .28 correlation, equally strong in the opposite direction. Focusing on the authoritative leadership style, we find that it has a .54 correlation with rewards –

strongly positive – and a .21 correlation with responsibility – positive, but not as strong. In other words, the style's correlation with rewards was more than twice that with responsibility.

According to the data, the authoritative leadership style has the most positive effect on climate, but three others – affiliative, democratic, and coaching – follow close behind. That said, the research indicates that no style should be relied on exclusively, and all have at least short-term uses.

Drivers of Climate.") Further, when we looked at the impact of climate on financial results – such as return on sales, revenue growth, efficiency, and profitability – we found a direct correlation between the two. Leaders who used styles that positively affected the climate had decidedly better financial results than those who did not. That is not to say that organizational climate is the only driver of performance. Economic conditions

| | Coercive | Authoritative | Affiliative | Democratic | Pacesetting | Coaching |
|---|---|---|---|---|---|---|
| Flexibility | -.28 | .32 | .27 | .28 | -.07 | .17 |
| Responsibility | -.37 | .21 | .16 | .23 | .04 | .08 |
| Standards | .02 | .38 | .31 | .22 | -.27 | .39 |
| Rewards | -.18 | .54 | .48 | .42 | -.29 | .43 |
| Clarity | -.11 | .44 | .37 | .35 | -.28 | .38 |
| Commitment | -.13 | .35 | .34 | .26 | -.20 | .27 |
| Overall impact on climate | -.26 | .54 | .46 | .43 | -.25 | .42 |

## The Affiliative Style

"People come first" is the hallmark of Affiliative leadership. The coercive leader demands, "Do what I say," whereas the authoritative urges, "Come with me."

The affiliative style prioritizes the team over tasks and goals. But you must avoid the habit of "people-pleasing," which can be destructive. The affiliative leadership style prioritizes emotional connections and harmony within a team. The goal is to foster positive relationships and create a supportive work environment. These leaders are empathetic and attentive to the emotional needs of their team members, promoting collaboration and unity. They excel in building strong interpersonal bonds, often encouraging open communication and team cohesion. While this approach can enhance morale and loyalty, it can also lead to challenges if overused, such as neglecting performance standards or avoiding necessary conflict.

The affiliative style is particularly effective in times of change or stress, as it helps to create a stable and trusting atmosphere where employees feel valued and motivated to contribute. The affiliative leadership style doesn't impose unnecessary restrictions on how employees get their work done. It gives people the freedom to do their work in the way they choose. This works well for some staff but can cause trouble for those who need more boundaries.

Affiliative leaders are masterful at creating a climate of belonging and positive feedback.

**Example:**

**Joe Torre,** former Manager of the New York Yankees, is a classic affiliative leader. During the 1999 World Series, Torre tended ably to the psyches of his players as they endured the emotional pressure cooker of a pennant race. He made a special point to praise Scott Brosius, whose father had died during the season, for staying committed even as he mourned. At the celebration party after the team's final game, Torre sought out right fielder Paul O'Neill. Although he had received the news of his father's death that morning, O'Neill chose to play in the decisive game, and he burst into tears the moment it ended. Torre made a point of acknowledging O'Neill's struggle, calling him a "warrior."

Torre also used the spotlight of the Victory celebration to praise two players whose return the following year was threatened by contract disputes. He sent a clear message to the team and the owner that he valued the players immensely and too much to lose them.

Along with ministering to the emotions of his people, an affiliative leader may also tend to his own emotions openly. The year Tori's brother was near death awaiting a heart transplant, he shared his worries with his players. He also spoke candidly with the team about his treatment for prostate cancer.

Torre is a great example of the Affiliative style.

## Democratic Style

Democratic leadership emphasizes collaboration and active participation from team members. Leaders who adopt this approach value their team's input and ideas. They desire an environment where everyone feels heard and respected. This style encourages creativity and innovation and enhances team commitment. Team members are more likely to feel a sense of ownership over the outcomes.

Democratic leaders facilitate open discussions and encourage constructive feedback. They allow diverse perspectives to shape decisions. While this approach can lead to more well-rounded solutions, it may also result in slower decision-making due to the need for consensus. The democratic leadership style is particularly effective in environments that thrive on teamwork and collective problem-solving.

While the democratic leadership style promotes collaboration and inclusivity, it has significant drawbacks. Decision-making can become slow and cumbersome, relying on consensus-building and extensive discussions.

This can hinder progress, especially in situations that require quick responses or decisive action.

Additionally, the leader must manage differing opinions or conflicts within the team. Team members may become overly reliant on the group for decisions, stifling individual initiative and accountability. Where clear guidance is necessary, the democratic style may create confusion or dilute responsibility, ultimately impacting the team's efficiency and effectiveness.

**Example:**

In the early 20th century, a significant figure in the fight for civil rights emerged: **Mahatma Gandhi**. Known for his democratic leadership style, Gandhi believed in the power of collective decision-making and the strength of the people. During India's struggle for independence, he adopted an inclusive approach, fostering participation from diverse groups nationwide.

Gandhi organized the Salt March in 1930 as a response to the oppressive salt tax imposed by the British government. Rather than planning the march unilaterally, he consulted with fellow leaders, activists, and ordinary citizens to build a broad coalition. He encouraged everyone to join the movement, emphasizing that the fight for freedom was a shared responsibility. Gandhi sought input and feedback through community meetings and discussions, ensuring every voice mattered.

As they marched to the Arabian Sea to collect salt, thousands of Indians joined Gandhi, demonstrating the movement's collective strength. Along the way, he held gatherings to discuss their goals and strategies, ensuring that participants felt involved and invested in the cause. This democratic approach galvanized support and united people from different backgrounds, including peasants, workers, and intellectuals.

Gandhi's leadership style inspired a sense of ownership among his followers. His commitment to nonviolent resistance attracted international attention. By stimulating collaboration and encouraging input, he empowered individuals to believe that they could make a difference. His efforts played a crucial role in India's gaining independence in 1947, showcasing the power of democratic leadership in achieving social change and uniting a nation under a common cause.

## Pacesetting Style

The pacesetting leadership style is characterized by a leader who sets high-performance standards and expects excellence from their team. This approach focuses on achieving results quickly and efficiently. The leader leads by example, inspiring team members to match their energy and commitment. However, this approach should be used sparingly. The pacesetting style can destroy the workplace climate.

Pacesetting leaders are highly driven and detail-oriented. They push their teams to meet ambitious goals and deadlines. While this style can lead to impressive short-term gains and high productivity, it may also create a high-pressure environment that, if not managed carefully, can lead to burnout and decreased morale. A pacesetting leader's talk track may sound like, "If I have to tell you, you are the wrong person for the job."

Team members may feel overwhelmed by the expectations, leading to a lack of creativity and collaboration. The focus remains on meeting specific targets rather than fostering a supportive and innovative culture. Pacesetting leaders give little feedback on how people are doing. They may jump in to take over when they think the team is "lagging." If the leader leaves, people feel directionless. They've grown reliant on the leader setting the "rules."

While the pacesetting style can effectively achieve immediate results, leaders must balance their drive for excellence with the well-being of their team to sustain long-term success.

**Example:**

**Elon Musk**, the CEO of Tesla and SpaceX, embodies the pacesetting leadership style. Musk is known for his high expectations and relentless pursuit of innovation and efficiency. He sets ambitious goals, such as producing electric vehicles at unprecedented speeds and making space travel commercially viable.

Musk leads by example. He often works long hours, pushing his teams to match his intensity and commitment to excellence. During the ramp-up of Tesla's Model 3 production, Musk famously set a goal to achieve a production rate of five thousand cars per week. He was known to sleep at the factory and encourage his employees to adopt a similar work ethic.

This approach has led to significant advancements and rapid growth in his companies. However, it has also garnered criticism for creating a high-pressure environment, contributing to employee burnout, and raising concerns about work-life balance. Nonetheless, Musk's pacesetting leadership has driven innovation in the automotive and aerospace industries, solidifying his reputation as a transformative figure in business.

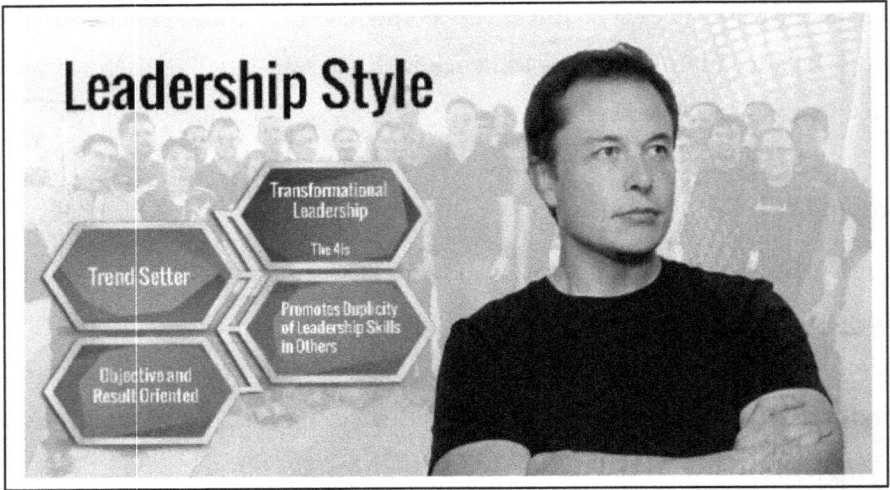

Leadership Style

Transformational Leadership

The 4 Is

Trend Setter

Promotes Duplicity of Leadership Skills in Others

Objective and Result Oriented

## The Coaching Style

The coaching leadership style focuses on developing individuals and teams. These leaders foster personal and professional growth through guidance and support. They prioritize building strong relationships with their team members, taking the time to understand their strengths, weaknesses, and aspirations. Research has shown that it's the least used of the six styles.[50] Most leaders say they don't have time to slow down, teach people, and help them grow. What a shame! Leaders who bypass this are missing out on a secret weapon. The impact of the coaching style on climate and performance is markedly positive.

By providing constructive feedback and encouragement, coaching leaders empower employees to improve their skills and achieve their goals. This approach emphasizes open communication, active listening, and collaborative problem-solving. It creates an environment where team members feel safe to express themselves and take risks. When implemented effectively, coaching leadership can enhance overall performance, boost confidence, and cultivate a culture of continuous organizational learning and development.

The coaching style must be revised when employees have a fixed mindset or resist learning or changing their ways. It will also fail if the leader lacks the knowledge or skills to coach. Although this style may not immediately scream "bottom line results," it can deliver them.

**Example:**

**Satya Nadella,** Microsoft's CEO, exemplifies the coaching leadership style. When Nadella took the helm in 2014, he recognized the need for a cultural transformation within the company, shifting its focus from a competitive, siloed environment to one that prioritizes collaboration and growth. He promotes a "growth mindset," encouraging employees to learn from failures and continuously improve their skills.

Nadella is known for his commitment to coaching, mentorship, and connecting with employees at all levels. He fosters open communication and encourages team members to share ideas and feedback, creating a culture of trust and support. Under his leadership, Microsoft has emphasized the importance of personal development, providing resources and opportunities for employees to enhance their capabilities. This coaching approach has revitalized the company's culture and contributed to Microsoft's impressive growth and innovation in recent years, demonstrating coaching leadership's effectiveness in driving individual and organizational success.

# Expand Your Repertoire

To be the most successful leader, you must exhibit **several styles**. When you master four or more of these particular leadership styles, especially authoritative, democratic, affiliative, and coaching styles, you will create the best climate and performance in your business.

It's not about making a mechanical effort to fit into a specific checklist of items that one or more match. You must be fluid and sensitive to your particular organization and then be able to adjust continually to get the best results.

The "law of the lid" holds that the greater your flexibility and ability to utilize different strategies, the more wins you'll have.

*PROTIP*: It's common to think you won't be able to incorporate all these styles; however, consider building your leadership team with members who can employ the styles you lack.

You may need to expand your repertoire of leadership styles. To do so, you must understand which emotional intelligence competencies underlie the leadership style you lack. You can then work diligently to increase your percentage of them.

### Emotional Intelligence for Leaders

Expanding your repertoire is essential for effective leadership in today's dynamic and diverse workplace. Emotional intelligence (EI) serves as a crucial underpinning in this development, allowing leaders to adapt their approach based on the needs of their team and the context in which they operate. By cultivating key emotional intelligence competencies, leaders can enhance their ability to switch between styles, such as affiliative, pacesetting, or authoritative, thereby becoming more versatile and effective in guiding their teams.

For example, Affiliative leaders excel in empathy, relationship-building, and communication. Their capacity to sense and respond to the emotional states of team members creates an environment of trust and collaboration. To leverage this style more effectively, a pacesetting leader—who typically focuses on achieving high performance and fast results—must develop their emotional intelligence, particularly in empathy and interpersonal communication. By enhancing these skills, the pacesetting leader can learn to connect with team members and understand their challenges and motivations. This connection can soften the high-pressure environment often accompanying a pacesetting approach and promote a more supportive and collaborative atmosphere where employees feel valued and understood.

Similarly, an authoritative leader looking to incorporate democratic leadership traits should focus on building competencies in collaboration and communication. While authoritative leaders set a clear vision and direction, incorporating democratic elements values team members' input and ideas. Authoritative leaders can create a more inclusive environment by enhancing their skills in active listening and encouraging open dialogue. This shift allows team members to feel empowered and engaged in decision-making.

Adding new capabilities may seem straightforward, but enhancing emotional intelligence requires intentional practice and self-reflection. Leaders can engage in various developmental activities, such as seeking feedback from colleagues, participating in workshops focused on emotional intelligence, and actively reflecting on their interactions with team members.

Through consistent effort and practice, leaders can successfully expand their repertoire of leadership styles, ultimately enhancing their effectiveness and the overall success of their teams. This continuous journey of self-improvement strengthens individual leadership capabilities and cultivates a more resilient and adaptive organizational culture.

*For more information on how to improve your emotional intelligence, see the section on EQ and consider enrolling in our Lead360 Course, which delivers bite-sized EQ and other impactful help to leaders.*

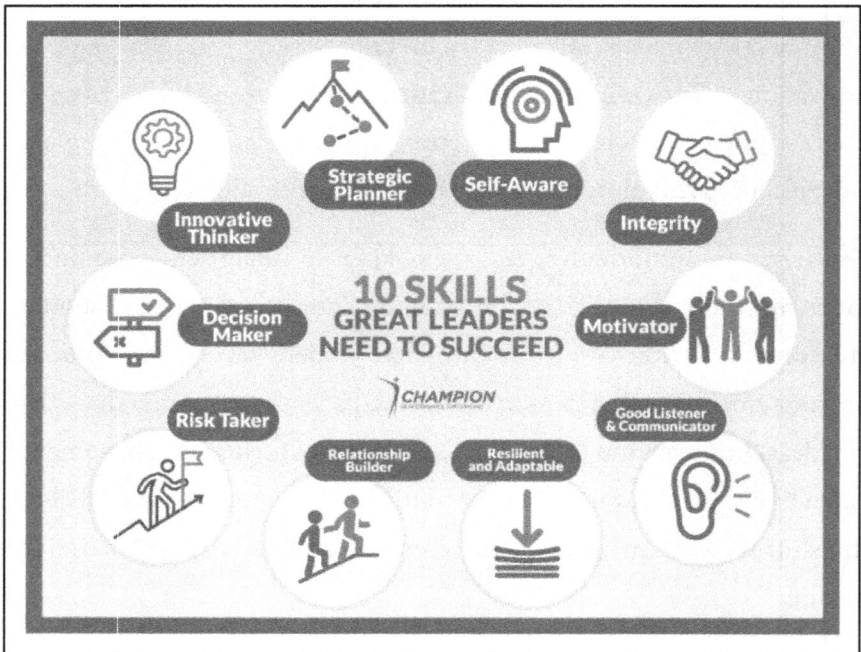

## Top Skills for Leadership - The Ten Skills Of Great Leaders

A diverse set of skills is crucial for navigating the complexities of guiding a team. So, what are the top ten skills that define great leaders? These skills are the backbone of effective leadership, enabling leaders to inspire and motivate their teams while adapting and innovating in an ever-evolving environment. By mastering these competencies, leaders can make informed decisions, build cohesive teams, and communicate clearly and purposefully. Can you cultivate them to elevate your leadership potential and drive meaningful impact within your organization?

## 1. Self-Awareness

Mastering the art of emotional regulation is a key component to becoming a standout leader. As leaders, the ability to navigate emotions, manage stress, and maintain composure under pressure is not just beneficial—it is essential. These skills help leaders handle the complexities of modern workplaces, where the pace of change and the demands on time and resources are ever-increasing. No matter the industry, everyone encounters potential roadblocks. Strong leadership can successfully overcome many difficulties.

For me, becoming a great leader did not happen overnight. I was not born a leader; I learned by experience. At twenty-five years old, I was in a C-suite role, managing six locations of a thriving dental business with hundreds of employees and multiple partners. As COO, I was the regional manager of operations. My duties were extensive. Managing people with different dynamics, personalities, and backgrounds was the biggest challenge.

At first, the team didn't accept my leadership. They didn't want to be led by a young "baby executive," as they called me. They had a valid point. I was the youngest member of the leadership team by eighteen years. In the employee's eyes, I had much to learn. However, they underestimated the power of my grit, tenacity, and drive, all benefits of my growth and owner mindset.

I was persistent and hungry to learn every aspect of my position and then some. I went to outside courses and obtained one-on-one coaching to become the leader I knew I could be. I worked at this daily, growing by leaps and bounds. My leadership growth sparked growth in the business. Remembering these moments makes me think of John C. Maxwell's concept of "The Law of the Lid."

John C. Maxwell's idea of "The Law of the Lid" is a foundational principle in his comprehensive exploration of leadership. This law states that a person's leadership ability is a lid or cap on their effectiveness. In essence, the lower an individual's ability to lead, the lower the lid on their potential success. Conversely, as leadership skills improve, so does the potential for personal and organizational success. This principle highlights the critical nature of leadership development, suggesting that one's ability to lead effectively can be the primary determinant of success in any endeavor.

For example, a manager who struggles with communication and delegation may find their team underperforming, whereas a manager who excels in these areas can inspire and drive their team to new heights. Improving leadership skills raises this lid, unleashing greater potential for achievement and growth. Individuals can enhance their influence and impact by developing key leadership competencies, such as emotional intelligence, strategic thinking, and the ability to inspire and motivate others.

Consider a small business owner who handles all aspects of the business themselves. As they cultivate leadership skills, such as delegation and team-building, they empower their team to take on more responsibilities, increasing productivity and innovation. This transformation boosts the business's success and fosters a more dynamic and engaged work environment. This clearly illustrates the profound impact of raising your leadership lid. I experienced this firsthand as I developed my skills and observed the same growth within my team.

**Example: The Law of the Lid**

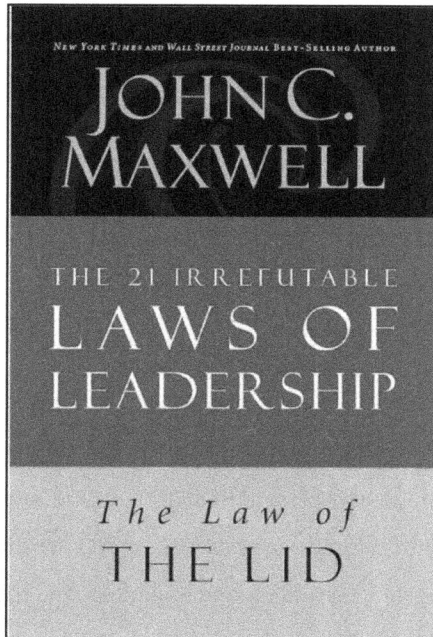

In 1937, two young brothers, Dick and Maurice McDonald, opened a small drive-in restaurant in Pasadena, California. The little restaurant was a hit. In 1940, they moved the operation to San Bernardino, a booming working-class town fifty miles east of Los Angeles. The business thrived, with annual sales hitting $200,000—an impressive sum back then.

In 1948, they revamped the business. They streamlined operations, reduced their menu to focus on hamburgers, and introduced what they called the "Speedy Service System." Their kitchen functioned like an assembly line, with each employee focused on speed. Their goal was to fulfill each customer's order in 30 seconds or less, and they succeeded. By the 1950s, revenue had soared to $350,000, and the brothers split net profits of around $100,000 annually. Dick and Maurice McDonald had struck gold, but they didn't take it any further. Their lack of leadership put a ceiling on their success.

The McDonald brothers were geniuses in customer service and kitchen efficiency. They created a system that revolutionized the food industry. But when they attempted to expand in 1952, they failed. The reason? **They lacked the leadership needed to grow beyond a single successful restaurant.** While they were excellent managers—skilled in running an efficient business, cutting costs, and increasing profits—they were *not* visionaries. Their thinking held them back, and they hit the "Law of the Lid."

In 1954, Ray Kroc entered the picture. When he visited their store, he immediately saw the potential for nationwide expansion. In his mind, McDonald's could be everywhere. He struck a deal with the brothers, and in 1955, he formed McDonald's Systems, which would later become the McDonald's Corporation. Under Kroc's leadership, the company soared. Between 1955 and 1959, Kroc opened a hundred restaurants; four years later, that number had grown to five hundred. In 1961, for $2.7 million, Kroc bought the exclusive rights to McDonald's from the brothers, transforming it into a global institution.

This story highlights the importance of the "Law of the Lid." The McDonald brothers had the talent to build something great but needed more leadership to take it further. Ray Kroc, on the other hand, had the vision and leadership to elevate McDonald's to unprecedented heights. Leadership, not just management, made all the difference. As a leader, your job is to help your team to develop these skills.

As I became a better leader, my team's confidence increased. Their doubt and insecurities diminished as I continued to rise to the occasion. I was solving problems and guiding their transformation as I evolved and transformed. My emotional regulation skills proved invaluable in navigating personal and professional challenges. Whether I was dealing with high-pressure deadlines at work or unexpected personal setbacks, maintaining emotional control allowed me to think clearly and make rational decisions.

Once, we faced a critical project at work. Tensions were high, and conflicts arose among team members. My ability to stay calm and composed helped diffuse the situation, enabling us to refocus on our common goals and complete the project successfully. Similarly, in personal relationships, managing my emotions prevented misunderstandings and fostered healthier communication. This emotional resilience enhanced my leadership and inspired confidence and trust among those around me, leading to stronger connections and more effective teamwork.

Emotional regulation is integral to self-awareness. Self-aware leaders better understand their emotional responses and how they affect decision-making and communication. This self-awareness is the foundation upon which emotional intelligence is built, allowing leaders to empathize with others, build trust, and create an inclusive environment. Through the development of emotional intelligence, leaders can significantly improve their effectiveness and build better team dynamics by understanding and valuing different perspectives.

By mastering these skills, leaders can inspire team confidence and encourage open communication and collaboration. Strong relationships and a supportive atmosphere result when leaders connect with their teams on an emotional level, driving organizational success. This emotional connection is crucial for motivating employees, enhancing engagement, and aligning their efforts with organizational goals. As leaders, we are always "working for the team." Being a servant leader fosters a positive work environment, enhances collaboration, and boosts employee satisfaction and business performance.

Moreover, emotional regulation transforms challenges into opportunities for growth and innovation. Leaders who approach obstacles calmly are better equipped to develop creative solutions and navigate challenges. This ability not only aids in tackling current challenges but also strengthens the team's resilience, equipping them to handle future uncertainties.

## 2. Authenticity & Integrity

What does leading with authenticity and integrity mean? Why is it important? Leading with authenticity and integrity is about staying true to your values and beliefs while guiding others. Authentic leaders are genuine, approachable, and consistent in their actions, which builds trust and respect among team members. Being transparent and open creates an environment where everyone feels safe to express their ideas and concerns. This kind of leadership encourages individuals to bring their true selves to work. Authentic leaders inspire others to follow suit, leading to a more cohesive and motivated team.

My teams feel "safe" with me because I stay true to myself in all interactions. I consistently present myself authentically when engaging with leaders, team members, or clients. This feels natural to me. It's something I've carried throughout my life. It started with my parents' example. Every decision and action they made in business was built on being true to themselves and operating with conviction and honesty. My parents never changed who they were and what they stood for. Their example inspired my business style, consistently guiding my professional interactions and decisions and reinforcing the trust and safety my teams rely on. My parents initially shaped my leadership style, but seasoned leaders guided my growth and aspirations.

I've observed many leaders who naturally embody authenticity and integrity, guiding their companies and making business decisions based on their core values. They never waver from these principles, always speaking and living by the truth. These leaders have greatly influenced my approach, reinforcing the belief that being genuine fosters trust and respect. This authenticity enhances team dynamics, creating an environment where everyone feels valued and motivated. By staying true to my values, I contribute to a positive organizational culture where transparency and honesty pave the way for collective success.

Integrity in leadership means making decisions aligned with your and your organization's core values and maintaining consistency between words and actions. Leaders with integrity are reliable and honest. They strengthen their credibility with those they lead. This quality is crucial for building an organizational culture where ethical behavior is valued and expected.

Leaders who act with integrity set the standard for acceptable behavior and influence the organization's overall behavior. Leadership grounded in authenticity and integrity paves the way for long-term success by strengthening a stable and committed workforce aligned with the organization's mission and goals.

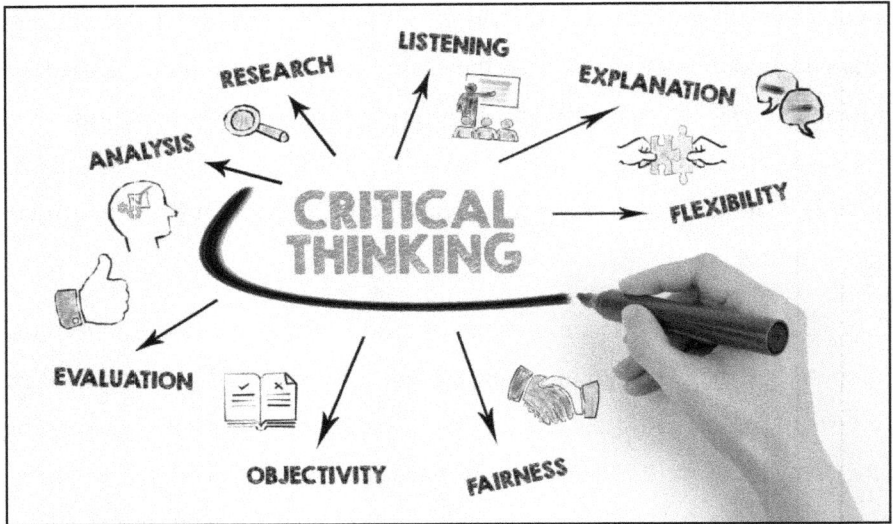

## 3. Critical Thinking

Critical thinking sets great leaders apart, empowering them to navigate the complexities of their roles with precision and insight. Critical thinking enables leaders to analyze complex situations by breaking them down into manageable components, allowing for a clear understanding of the factors at play. This skill is crucial for making informed decisions, as it involves evaluating information objectively and considering it from multiple angles. This helps leaders anticipate potential challenges and devise strategic solutions to achieve immediate and long-term goals.

The ability to solve problems effectively is paramount. Critical thinking allows leaders to remain calm and composed under pressure, examining issues methodically rather than reacting impulsively. This thoughtful approach leads to better decision-making and stimulates innovation. By questioning assumptions and exploring alternative solutions, leaders can drive their teams toward creative breakthroughs that might remain undiscovered.

I had a singular goal when I wrote my first book and developed my training programs: **to lead dental teams to achieve professional excellence.** I wanted to lead readers on a journey to boost leadership skills, strengthen team dynamics, and encourage innovation and growth in the dental industry. I needed to keep my critical thinking sharp to hit my goals and help teams and businesses succeed.

In *"Hygienepreneur: The Dental Hygienist's Guide to Achieving Career Success and Personal Transformation,"* critical thinking is vital in shaping leadership strategies for dental hygienists. When writing this book, I dove into the complexities of the dental field; I identified key leadership opportunities that empower hygienists to ascend into influential roles. This involved a thorough analysis of industry dynamics and leadership demands. This research enabled the development of frameworks to support hygienists in becoming leaders who drive change and innovation.

One notable application of critical thinking is emphasizing leadership through collaboration and mentorship. My book encourages hygienists to adopt a leadership style that fosters team empowerment and collective growth by challenging traditional hierarchical structures. This approach enhances their impact and cultivates a supportive environment that inspires others to excel.

The book provides insights into how critical thinking can help hygienists navigate leadership challenges ranging from managing diverse teams to spearheading public health initiatives. Hygienists can lead confidently and clearly through strategic decision-making and effective communication techniques. These innovative approaches enable them to influence positive outcomes in their workplaces and communities.

Ultimately, the " The Hygienepreneur" brand leverages critical thinking to inspire dental hygienists to embrace their potential as leaders. By providing tools and strategies grounded in thoughtful analysis, the book empowers them to lead within dental offices and broader healthcare and entrepreneurial contexts, fostering a new generation of leaders in the dental industry. I first shared a success plan with these teams by using my critical thinking and encouraging theirs, helping them thrive in and outside of the company.

Critical thinking also enhances strategic planning by enabling leaders to foresee potential obstacles and opportunities. It encourages a forward-thinking mindset that prioritizes adaptability and proactive measures. Leaders who cultivate critical thinking can guide their organizations through uncertain times, ensuring resilience and continued growth.

To develop critical thinking, leaders should engage in activities that challenge their reasoning abilities, such as debates, scenario analysis, and reflective practices. Encouraging open dialogue and diverse viewpoints within their teams also broadens their perspective, nurturing a culture of continuous learning and improvement. By honing their critical thinking skills, leaders elevate their effectiveness, inspire confidence in their decision-making, and lead their organizations well.

## 4. Adaptability

Great leaders are adaptable. Adaptability is crucial in navigating the ever-changing landscape of business. Continuous learning keeps you informed and ready for new challenges. This is key to embracing adaptability. Adaptability lets you pivot effectively when unexpected situations arise. These leaders don't shy away from setbacks but instead view them as opportunities for growth. They actively encourage feedback from their teams, fostering a culture of collaboration and innovation. Adaptability helps you steer your organization through turbulent times and inspire your teams to remain agile and proactive, ultimately driving long-term success. Leaders must sometimes be comfortable with the uncomfortable to grow and prosper.

Once, I worked with an amazing team in Virginia, where I met an inspiring office manager facing some hurdles with adaptability. Leading a dynamic group and navigating a new owner refining his leadership, she had quite the challenge. The responsibility for the business's growth was hers to bear; she felt that it was all on her shoulders.

At first, she encountered a lot of pushback. Her team was skeptical about her ideas and frequently challenged her suggestions. Her resilience amidst these trials stood out to me. Initially, she feared stepping out of her comfort zone—a vital quality for effective leadership—but she was willing to learn and evolve.

We concentrated on bolstering her leadership and sharpening her adaptability. We used strategies like welcoming change instead of resisting it, actively gathering feedback from her team, and committing to ongoing learning to stay at the forefront of industry developments. She began to see challenges as stepping stones for innovation and growth.

We introduced her to scenario planning, enabling her to foresee various outcomes and prepare accordingly. This approach elevated her confidence and encouraged her team to trust her decision-making. She initiated regular brainstorming sessions, inviting team members to share their thoughts and ideas, nurturing a culture of collaboration.

By the conclusion of our training, her transformation was undeniable. Her newfound adaptability became central to her leadership style, inspiring her team and propelling the business toward success. Stories like these illustrate the profound impact of adaptability in leadership—it's about more than just managing change; it's about flourishing because of it.

## 5. Inspiration and Persuasion

Mastering the skills of inspiration and persuasion transforms your leadership style and how your team perceives and responds to you. These skills are the cornerstone of effective leadership, enabling you to inspire your team, motivate individuals to reach their full potential and persuade stakeholders to align with common goals. Inspiration sparks the true potential within.

### Inspiration

*"Influence is the ability to inspire action."* - **Rory Vaden**

When a leader or manager has genuine influence, their team willingly follows, not because they're commanded to, but because they are inspired to do so.

Many leaders need to pay more attention to the foundational work of building influence or inspiration. They may assume that when their words fail or their team doesn't immediately comply, the solution is to resort to manipulation, fear, or anger.

But true leadership doesn't come from force. It comes from *earning the right to be followed*. To inspire your team, you must first prove you're worth following. Here are the four key foundations of becoming an inspirational leader:

*Mutual Trust:* Your team must trust that you understand and respect their challenges. Words may go unheard when they don't come from a place of empathy and shared experience. Building trust means listening, showing genuine empathy, and rolling up your sleeves before expecting your team to succeed.

*Strong Relationships:* Inspirational leaders don't succeed in isolation. They actively seek help and build relationships at all levels. Rather than standing above others, they collaborate and cultivate strong connections with key stakeholders, fostering a support network.

*Hard Work:* Actions speak louder than words. To be an inspirational leader, you must model the behavior and work ethic you want to see in your team. You become someone they aspire to emulate through what you say and what you do.

*Positive Influence:* True influence isn't about manipulation or coercion. It's about demonstrating value to those around and above you. When you're inspirational, it becomes easier to secure resources, take on exciting projects, and create new opportunities for your team.

Inspiration is about lighting a fire within your team and helping them see the bigger picture and their role in it.

### The Do's and Don'ts of Inspiring Your Team

Many leaders struggle with building influence and inspiration. When they get it wrong, the entire team suffers. Common mistakes include overemphasizing one aspect of leadership while neglecting others. Some leaders focus too much on gaining influence and building relationships with those above them, leaving their teams overworked and unsupported. Others skip the trust-building process, failing to truly listen to their team.

To be an inspirational leader, you must carefully balance all four foundations: trust, relationships, hard work, and influence. This balance requires strong empathy, leadership skills, and effective time management.

As you work toward becoming an inspiring leader, keep these critical do's and don'ts in mind:

*Do's:*

- **Listen actively** to your team to build trust and understanding.
- **Foster relationships** at all levels, both within your team and beyond.
- **Lead by example**, showing your team the work ethic and commitment you expect from them.
- **Advocate for your team**, ensuring they have the resources and opportunities to succeed.

*Don'ts:*

- **Don't neglect trust-building**, assuming your team will follow without true connection.
- **Don't over-focus** on pleasing higher-ups at the expense of your team's well-being.
- **Don't rely solely** on words to inspire—your actions must back them up.
- **Don't avoid collaboration;** thinking leadership is about working in isolation or making unilateral decisions.

| 👍 Do | 👎 Don't |
|---|---|
| Build authentic relationships with the people you work with. | Create one-way or manipulative relationships that only benefit you. |
| Show that you listen and care about what your teammates say. | Use "I" too much when talking to your team or about ideas. |
| Be open to hearing constructive criticism and improving on your weaknesses. | Close yourself off to criticism or outrightly dismiss constructive feedback. |
| Stay consistent in your approach and support those around you to build trust. | Be flaky. If you're unreliable, people won't trust you or follow you. |
| Invest in building your own expertise. The best way to inspire is to be inspirational. | Get lazy and think you know everything. Those who inspire are lifelong learners. |
| Bring others with you on the journey. The best leaders are those who build others up. | Push people aside or use them solely to progress your own career. |
| Work on your body language to convey a confident and approachable demeanor. | Close yourself off from others, either in your approach or your attitude. |

To cultivate this skill, consider these exercises:

- **Vision Crafting:** Spend time articulating your vision for the team or project. Communicate this vision clearly and passionately, ensuring everyone understands their part in the journey. Create vision boards to make them tangible and relatable to the team.

- **Storytelling Sessions:** Share stories of past successes or challenges overcome. Stories have the power to connect emotionally with your team, making the vision more relatable and inspiring.

## Persuasion: Aligning Stakeholders and Teams

Effective leadership is more than just giving directives—it's inspiring others to take action through influence. Persuasion is one of the most powerful tools in a leader's arsenal. It guides others toward a desired outcome while furthering collaboration and trust. Leaders who master persuasion don't rely on authority; instead, they communicate their vision in ways that resonate with their team's needs and values.

**Key Elements of Persuasive Leadership:**

- *Empathy:* Persuasive leaders understand their audience's concerns, motivations, and challenges. By actively listening and showing empathy, they can frame their message to align with the team's values.

- *Credibility:* Trust is essential for persuasion. Leaders who demonstrate competence, consistency, and integrity earn the respect and confidence of their teams. People who believe in the leader are likely to buy into their ideas.

- *Logic and Evidence:* Presenting clear, logical arguments supported by data or real-world examples helps leaders build a strong case. When people see a logical connection between the goal and the action, they're more inclined to support it.

- *Emotional Appeal:* Persuasion often goes beyond logic. Effective leaders know how to appeal to emotions. They paint a compelling vision that sparks enthusiasm, pride, and a sense of purpose within the team.

- *Collaboration:* Persuasion isn't about one-sided communication. Great leaders engage in dialogue, seek input, and encourage participation. This collaborative approach fosters buy-in and a shared commitment to success.

By mastering persuasion, leaders can move people toward collective goals in an empowering and inclusive way. Instead of pushing or forcing outcomes, they create an environment where others feel motivated to follow their lead.

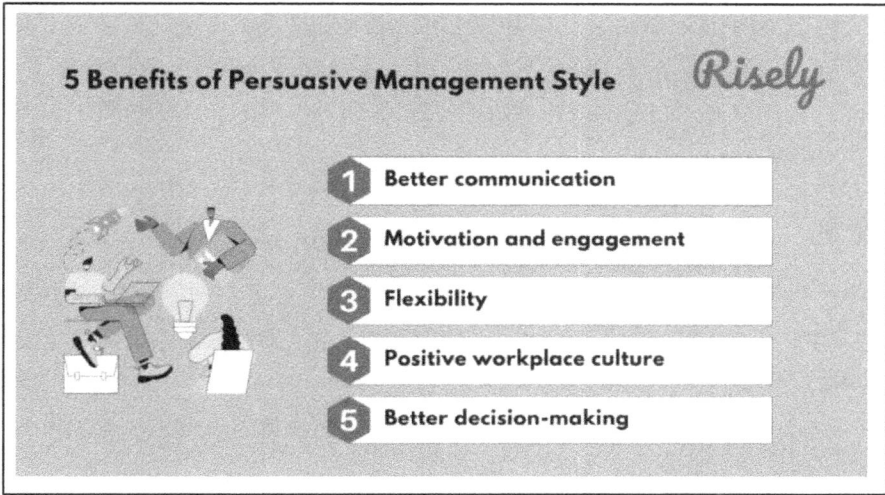

**5 Benefits of Persuasive Management Style**    *Risely*

1. Better communication
2. Motivation and engagement
3. Flexibility
4. Positive workplace culture
5. Better decision-making

## Bolstering Your Persuasive Abilities

- *Active Listening Exercises:* Practice active listening in meetings. Ensure you understand others' perspectives before presenting your ideas. This builds trust and makes your arguments more compelling.

- **Role-Playing Scenarios:** Engage in role-playing exercises where you and your team simulate negotiations or presentations. This helps refine your ability to present compelling arguments and respond effectively to counterarguments.

## Practical Exercises for Growth

To grow these skills further, integrate these practical exercises into your routine:

- *Daily Reflection:* At the end of each day, reflect on your interactions with the team. Consider what went well and what could be improved. Use these reflections to adjust your approach and strategies.

- *Feedback Loops:* Establish a culture of feedback where team members feel comfortable giving and receiving constructive criticism. This will improve team dynamics and enhance personal growth.

In the workplace, inspiration requires transparency and openness. Developing the skills of inspiration, motivation, and persuasion requires commitment and practice. Focusing on these areas will enhance your leadership capabilities and foster an environment where your team thrives. Remember, great leaders are not born but made through continuous learning and adaptation.

## 6. Negotiation

There isn't a day in a workplace that doesn't require the art and science of smooth finesse or negotiation. We are constantly negotiating, whether we realize it or not. From discussing what kind of coffee we'd prefer to order for the breakroom to negotiating a salary for an existing employee, a strategic partnership, or making an offer to a new employee, whether that is negotiating for a better rate from a vendor or presenting various options to a customer or patient, negotiation is a part of everything.

### Getting Out of "Black & White" Thinking

Black-and-white thinking is a cognitive pattern leading individuals to see things as absolutes. For example, one might feel they will get what they want in the negotiation or walk away. Psychologists view this pattern as a **cognitive distortion** because it prevents us from recognizing life's complexity, uncertainty, and constant change. This rigid mindset hinders our ability to find a middle ground, making it difficult to navigate life effectively.

Cognitive distortions are biased thoughts that create negative patterns in a person's thinking. They can be a response to depression and anxiety[36] Go into negotiations with a flexible approach to your thoughts so you can move away from "all or nothing" statements. These statements contribute to negative feelings without considering their accuracy. Cognitive techniques can help us identify these thought patterns and challenge our distorted perceptions.

**PROTIP:** See the emotional intelligence section of the book to review cognitive techniques for identifying thought patterns.

Know that negotiation doesn't mean giving in. When you negotiate to buy a new car, you're not giving in – you're bargaining. Keep in mind that negotiating is not about winning and losing. It's about getting the best outcome.

**Consider How Both Parties Can WIN**

Approaching a negotiation with a growth mindset means focusing on collaboration and finding solutions where both parties can win. If a long-time employee requests a significant raise, the boss can explore creative ways to meet her needs while protecting the company's financial health. Instead of viewing the raise as a fixed cost, the boss could propose performance-based incentives or additional benefits like professional development opportunities.

At the same time, the employee remains open to phased increases or new responsibilities. This mindset fosters mutual understanding and promotes outcomes that benefit both the employee's growth and the company's sustainability.

## Set Clear Boundaries and Objectives for the Negotiation

Define your priorities. Identify your non-negotiables and where you're willing to compromise. This gives you a clear purpose, allows you to communicate expectations to the other party, and provides a sense of confidence throughout the process. Organizing the negotiation with your interests in mind ensures you stay focused on your goals. Setting firm boundaries and pursuing well-defined objectives will make you more likely to reach a successful resolution.

## Prepare Clear and Reliable Information

Before entering a negotiation, make sure you have gathered accurate, well-supported data. Ask yourself, "What questions might arise? What are the key points?"

## Be Strategic and Kind

You want to be strategic. Consider their viewpoints. Being strategic in workplace negotiations is essential for long-term success, much like Napoleon Bonaparte, who planned meticulously before each battle to gain the upper hand. True victory in negotiation isn't just about tactics—it's about relationships. In *How to Win Friends and Influence People*, Dale Carnegie emphasizes the power of empathy, active listening, and mutual respect. Combining Napoleon's strategic mindset with Hill's focus on understanding and influencing others creates a balanced approach where you thoughtfully plan your moves while building trust and rapport to reach a win-win outcome.

**Be Genuine And Authentic While Listening Carefully**

Effective negotiation begins with building respect and rapport between all parties. When people feel valued and understood, they are more open to working together. Listen closely to what your counterpart is saying, and respond with sincerity.

As Kimbro Stakenas and Theodore Hirst noted in *Effective Negotiating*, "If we see our counterparts as people first and negotiators second, we'll unlock all kinds of doors." By showing genuine concern for your colleagues' well-being, you build trust and respect, making it easier to find mutually beneficial solutions. This is also the time to practice your active listening skills.

**Examine Your Internal Emotions And Feelings**

Take note of any emotions that arise when thinking about the negotiation process—tension, frustration, or excitement. These feelings can influence your strategy and the outcome, so it's essential to be aware of them. If needed, calm down or gather your energy before starting the negotiation. This ensures you stay composed and open-minded throughout the conversation.

In the workplace, emotions like frustration or a sense of unfairness—can cloud judgment. Expressing negative feelings may bring short-term results but can damage long-term relationships. Avoid reacting emotionally. Focus on using logic and calm persuasion. Before entering a difficult discussion, step back and process your emotions. Approach the situation clearly to communicate your concerns or demands effectively.

### Be Prepared To Compromise

No negotiation will ever go entirely in your favor. Be ready to make concessions. The other party may walk away if you're unwilling to compromise. A successful negotiation is one where both sides gain something. Before entering discussions, identify what you're willing to concede to achieve your short and long-term goals. Knowing your bottom line will help you recognize when walking away is best.

Many workplace disagreements can be avoided through compromise. Finding creative solutions that satisfy everyone may require effort, especially if your initial requests are rejected. Instead of reacting negatively or becoming passive-aggressive, understand your colleagues' perspectives and work towards counteroffers that benefit both parties. Rejections are opportunities to strengthen relationships and deepen your understanding of your colleagues.

### Be Assertive But Not Aggressive

In any negotiation, being confident in your position and clearly expressing your needs is important. Assertiveness allows you to communicate effectively without being overbearing. However, avoid crossing the line into aggression, which can create unnecessary tension and resistance.

I often advise clients to exercise caution when making work-related requests, even in leadership roles. Being overly aggressive can prompt pushback, even if your requests are reasonable.

This is especially true for those in positions of power, who may unintentionally come across as overbearing. Remember, a successful organization thrives on teamwork. Assertiveness is key to clear communication; aggression can lead to division. Focus on ethical tactics that influence others positively and advance cooperation.

### Maintain Perspective

When negotiating in the workplace, it's important to maintain perspective. Ask yourself, "Will this matter in a month, six months, a year, or even ten years?" This mindset helps you rise above the immediate tension and focus on the long run.

By considering the future impact of the negotiation, you can prioritize solutions that foster lasting relationships and long-term success rather than getting caught up in short-term wins or minor disagreements. This broader view helps keep emotions in check and encourages a more thoughtful, strategic approach to resolving conflicts.

## 7. Motivation and Team Building

Motivating a team is key to achieving organizational goals and enhancing productivity. When a team is motivated, they are more likely to be engaged in their work, which leads to higher-quality output and a more efficient workflow. Motivation fosters a positive environment where team members feel valued and driven to contribute their best efforts. This environment encourages individuals to exceed expectations and cultivates a culture of enthusiasm and commitment. Motivated teams collaborate more effectively. They overcome obstacles and innovate readily, driving the organization toward its objectives with a unified front.

One time, I sat down for a one-on-one brainstorming session with a team member named Lisa. She had always struck me as having a wealth of untapped potential. Despite Lisa's incredible ideas, she hadn't been nurtured to share them in the past. Seeing her gifts and creativity, I decided it was time to change that. I asked for her insight on enhancing our customer appointment scheduling process. She eagerly shared three big ideas that were pure gold. As we brainstormed, her input proved invaluable to our business.

Recognizing the brilliance of her ideas, I did what all great leaders should do—I delegated the project to her, encouraging her to take the lead and run with it. I expressed her amazing idea and emphasized its potential to pivot our business toward greater success. Lisa's excitement was palpable; being entrusted with the project gave her the power to lead and see it through. In that moment, she experienced personal and professional growth, becoming more engaged and passionate about her work. This experience reinforced the importance of motivation in leadership. Embracing it can transform lives.

As a leader, developing the ability to motivate is equally important. It directly influences employee satisfaction and turnover rates. A leader who can inspire their team nurtures a sense of belonging and purpose, which can significantly reduce turnover by fostering loyalty and commitment. Leaders build trust and rapport with their team by honing motivational skills and creating a foundation for open communication and collaboration.

Over time, this trust encourages innovation and risk-taking, as team members feel supported in their endeavors. Ultimately, the ability to motivate contributes to a cohesive team dynamic, laying the groundwork for sustained success and long-term growth within the organization.

### Driving the Team Forward

Motivation involves encouraging your team to push beyond their limits to achieve outstanding results. Here are some strategies to enhance your motivational skills:

- *Goal Setting:* Work with your team to set short-term and long-term goals. Ensure these goals are specific, measurable, achievable, relevant, and time-bound (SMART). Celebrate small wins to keep the momentum alive.

- *Recognition and Rewards:* Acknowledge individual and team achievements publicly. Implement a system of rewards that aligns with team values and encourages continued effort and dedication.

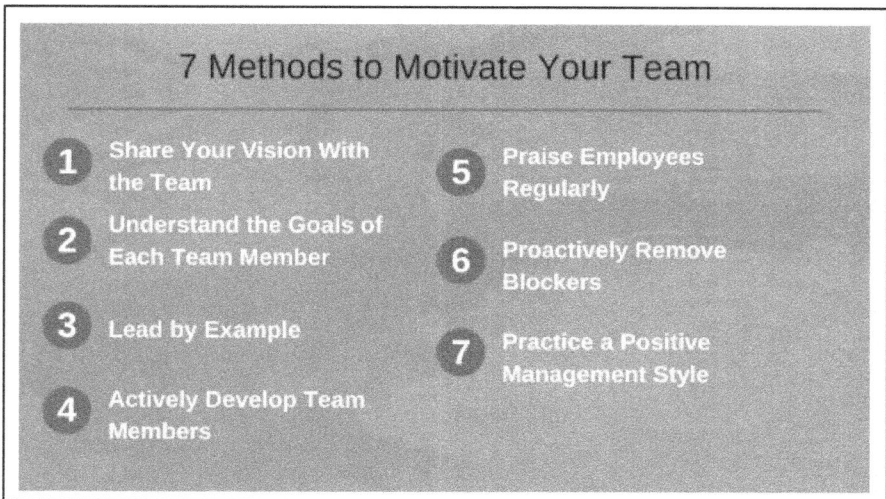

## 7 Methods to Motivate Your Team

1. Share Your Vision With the Team
2. Understand the Goals of Each Team Member
3. Lead by Example
4. Actively Develop Team Members
5. Praise Employees Regularly
6. Proactively Remove Blockers
7. Practice a Positive Management Style

## 8. Decision Making

Decision-making is a fundamental component of effective leadership. It's intricately linked to strategic thinking. Successful leaders must analyze information, evaluate options, and make informed choices that align with the organization's best interests. This requires balancing competing priorities and making necessary trade-offs.

Leaders must communicate their choices clearly and build support among their teams and stakeholders. Transparent communication builds trust and encourages buy-in, which are crucial for successfully implementing any decision.

Effective leaders excel at delegating responsibilities. They empower their team members to make decisions. This approach allows leaders to concentrate on critical tasks and strengthens and develops a capable team. Leaders can enhance overall organizational performance and resilience by fostering a sense of ownership among team members.

Leaders must assess the effectiveness of their decisions and learn from their experiences. This process of reflection and evaluation allows leaders to refine their decision-making skills over time, enhancing their overall effectiveness in their roles.

Leadership and decision-making are closely intertwined and critical for success in any organization or business. Effective leaders must think strategically, make well-informed decisions, communicate clearly, and commit to ongoing learning and growth. However, decision-making can be complex, and finding the right action can be challenging.

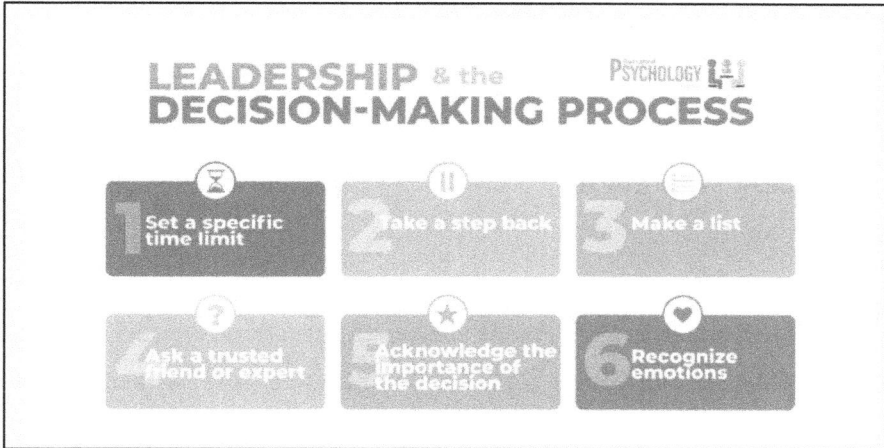

**LEADERSHIP** & the        **P**SYCHOLOGY
**DECISION-MAKING PROCESS**

1 Set a specific time limit

2 Take a step back

3 Make a list

4 Ask a trusted friend or expert

5 Acknowledge the importance of the decision

6 Recognize emotions

Steve Kerr, head coach of the Golden State Warriors, exemplifies real-world decision-making in sports leadership. Kerr is widely regarded for his strategic abilities on and off the court. His leadership and decision-making skills were displayed during the 2015 NBA Finals.

Kerr shifted his team's strategy. He moved Andre Iguodala into the starting lineup, benching their starting center. This was a bold move, as it meant playing a smaller lineup, commonly called "small ball." Kerr strategically analyzed the strengths and weaknesses of the Warriors' opponent, the Cleveland Cavaliers. He weighed the risks and benefits of the change.

This adjustment shifted the series' momentum, leading to the Warriors winning the championship. Kerr's ability to assess the situation, make an informed decision under pressure, and communicate the reasoning to his players exemplifies how strong decision-making is vital to leadership in sports and business. His willingness to adapt and take calculated risks contributed to the Warriors' success and solidified his reputation as a top coach in the league.

Five Key Elements to Effective Decision-Making

- *Clarity of Objectives:* Clearly define the goals and outcomes you want to achieve. Understanding the purpose behind your decision helps you focus on the best options that align with your business objectives.

- *Data-Driven Analysis:* Make your decisions based on accurate and relevant data. Collect and analyze information to understand the potential outcomes. Allow for informed and evidence-based decision-making.

- *Risk Assessment:* Evaluate the potential risks and rewards associated with each option. Understanding the short and long-term consequences helps mitigate risks and maximize opportunities.

- *Collaboration and Input:* Involve key stakeholders and team members in decision-making. Gather diverse perspectives to glean valuable insights, foster better decision-making, and build support for the final choice.

- *Decisiveness and Accountability:* Once a decision is made, act decisively and take ownership of the outcome. Strong leaders are accountable for their decisions, whether they succeed or fail, and they continuously evaluate and adjust as needed to ensure long-term success.

## 9. Influence

I remember having a coach in my twenties when I worked for a network marketing company. I was working for a supplement company and growing a team of sales leaders. Kevin Pine was not just a smooth talker; he was strategic and knew how to orchestrate. I always wished to have him in my head and use his words when I stumbled. One of the lessons he taught me was that we always orchestrate. We never manipulate; we always orchestrate. That was a huge key learning for me. He also taught me to "Envision the end before we begin." Stephen Covey. That was another huge learning for me. If you don't know where you are going, any road will lead you there.

To be truly effective, especially in both prosperous times and moments of great challenge, leaders must master the art of influencing others. Influence, by definition, is the ability to guide or shape the behavior of others toward a specific direction, using key strategies that engage, connect, and inspire those around them.

## Influencing People Varies by Role

In the early stages of your career or individual contributor roles, influence involves collaborating effectively with people you have no formal authority over. This requires logical, persuasive arguments and engaging in productive give-and-take.

As you move into mid-level leadership, the focus shifts to developing key skills needed to influence others. In senior or executive roles, influencing others centers on shaping long-term objectives, inspiring and motivating teams, and effectively communicating a vision.

No matter where you are in an organization, mastering the ability to influence others is essential for success.

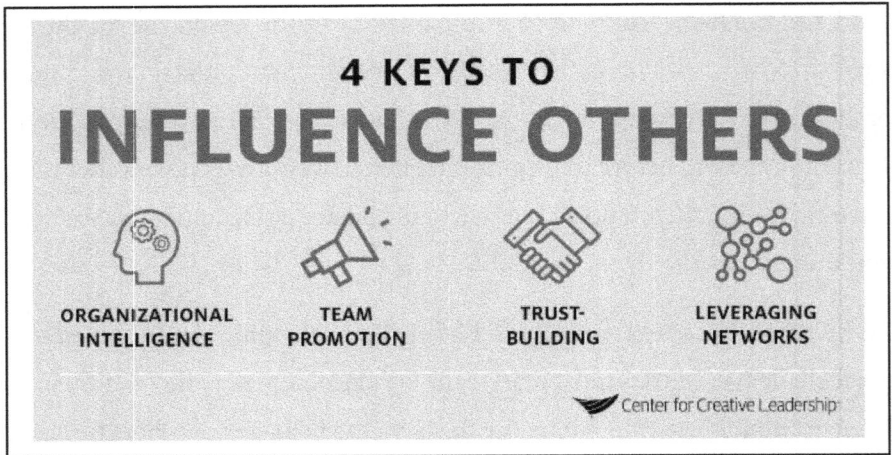

**4 KEYS TO**
# INFLUENCE OTHERS

ORGANIZATIONAL INTELLIGENCE | TEAM PROMOTION | TRUST-BUILDING | LEVERAGING NETWORKS

Center for Creative Leadership

According to the Centers for Creative Leadership, The best leaders have these four key influencing skills:[51]

**Organizational Intelligence: They understand how to get things done. They embrace the reality of working within organizational politics to move teams and important initiatives forward.**

Organizational Intelligence (OI) is critical for business leaders navigating the complexities of getting things done efficiently within a company. It refers to understanding, interpreting, and working with any organization's dynamics, structures, and politics.

For leaders, embracing OI means having a clear vision and knowing how to marshal the resources, relationships, and processes needed to bring that vision to life.

Understanding organizational politics is a key component of OI—acknowledging that personal interests, alliances, and power dynamics play a significant role in decision-making. Effective leaders leverage these realities, building influence across departments, fostering collaboration, and aligning diverse stakeholders toward common goals.

Rather than avoiding politics, they skillfully navigate them by establishing trust, communicating with transparency, and using their knowledge of the organizational landscape to anticipate challenges. By mastering the subtleties of OI, leaders can push critical initiatives forward with less friction, motivating teams and accelerating results while ensuring that the execution aligns with the company's strategic objectives and interpersonal dynamics.

**Team Promotion:** Leaders cut through the noise to authentically and credibly promote themselves and promote what's good for the entire organization.

## Promote Yourself, Elevate Your Team

Self-promotion often gets a bad reputation as boastful or self-serving. Leaders who understand the art of influence know that self-promotion is a powerful tool for standing out in a world of constant information overload. Self-promotion must be done authentically and for the right reasons,

In the hands of a skilled leader, authentic self-promotion goes beyond personal advancement. It brings visibility to the team's accomplishments, opens doors for direct reports, and builds pride within the organization. Leaders can foster greater collaboration and drive alignment across departments by highlighting their ideas and capabilities.

Two strategies of self-promotion are especially effective. First, influential leaders build an audience by involving more people in projects, initiatives, or problem-solving efforts. Second, they strategically "step into the spotlight" by creating or participating in key events and meetings, leveraging these opportunities to showcase their work and their team's contributions.

**Trust-Building**: Trust is essential because leadership often involves guiding people through risk and change. For leaders, building and sustaining trust is non-negotiable. They may get compliance without it, but they'll never unlock their team's full potential, commitment, or creativity. These qualities are essential when facing tough challenges or driving strategic change, making trust a critical asset.

People seek leaders who recognize their vulnerabilities, inspire confidence and support, and offer guidance through uncertainty. To foster trust, leaders must demonstrate a range of skills and behaviors. Some of these skills may seem contradictory, but when used wisely and at the right time, they create the conditions for trust to flourish.

Trust requires a delicate balance: pushing people outside their comfort zones while genuinely listening to their concerns and feedback. Trustworthy leaders master the art of balancing toughness with empathy during times of transition and urgency with patience as change unfolds, ensuring their teams feel supported and motivated even amidst uncertainty.

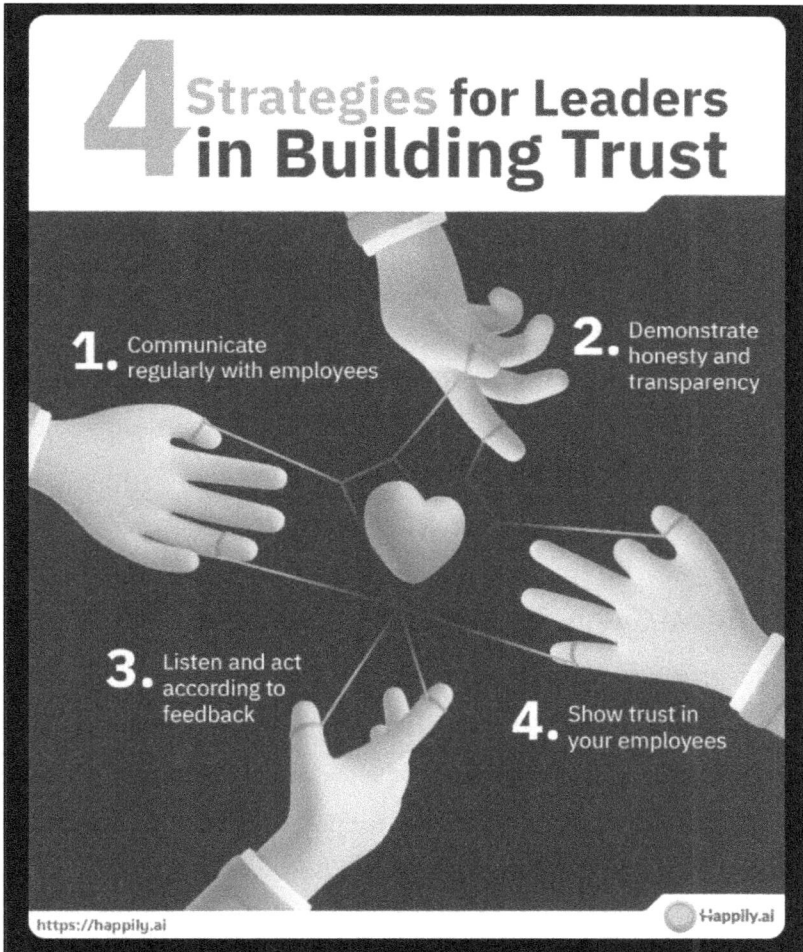

**4 Strategies for Leaders in Building Trust**

1. Communicate regularly with employees
2. Demonstrate honesty and transparency
3. Listen and act according to feedback
4. Show trust in your employees

https://happily.ai

Happily.ai

**Leveraging Networks:** No leader is "an island". Their connection with others empowers them. Leaders who excel at influencing others understand the immense power of networks and know how to leverage them effectively. A strong, adaptable network is essential in today's rapidly changing organizations, where teams, structures, and roles constantly evolve.

Savvy leaders maintain a "network perspective," recognizing that their connections must be as dynamic as the organization, continuously growing and evolving to meet new challenges and opportunities. These leaders don't just build relationships for the sake of it; they are intentional and strategic about expanding their networks, ensuring they are well-positioned to tap into diverse expertise, ideas, and resources when needed. They carefully consider how and when to engage their network, whether to solve complex problems, gather support for new initiatives, or drive collaboration across departments.

Influential leaders can navigate organizational changes more smoothly by fostering a broad, well-connected network, building bridges between different teams, and amplifying their impact, ensuring that they and their teams remain agile and well-equipped to tackle any challenge.

## 10. Political Savvy & Leadership Success

Do you consider yourself politically savvy at work? Individuals with political acumen tend to have better career prospects, are viewed as more promotable, and are less likely to experience career derailment. Those who bumble through or ignore the political realities of the workplace often miss out on valuable opportunities, connections, and resources.

Organizational politics are contentious and often uncomfortable but are a reality in every organization. Navigating them effectively is essential for success. Many leaders, particularly in large organizations, feel conflicted about engaging in political behavior. They may view it as manipulative or self-serving. Some see it as a necessary evil. Others reject it outright despite the potential negative impact on their careers. Political savvy is not inherently negative; it is a vital skill that can lead to positive outcomes for leaders and their teams.

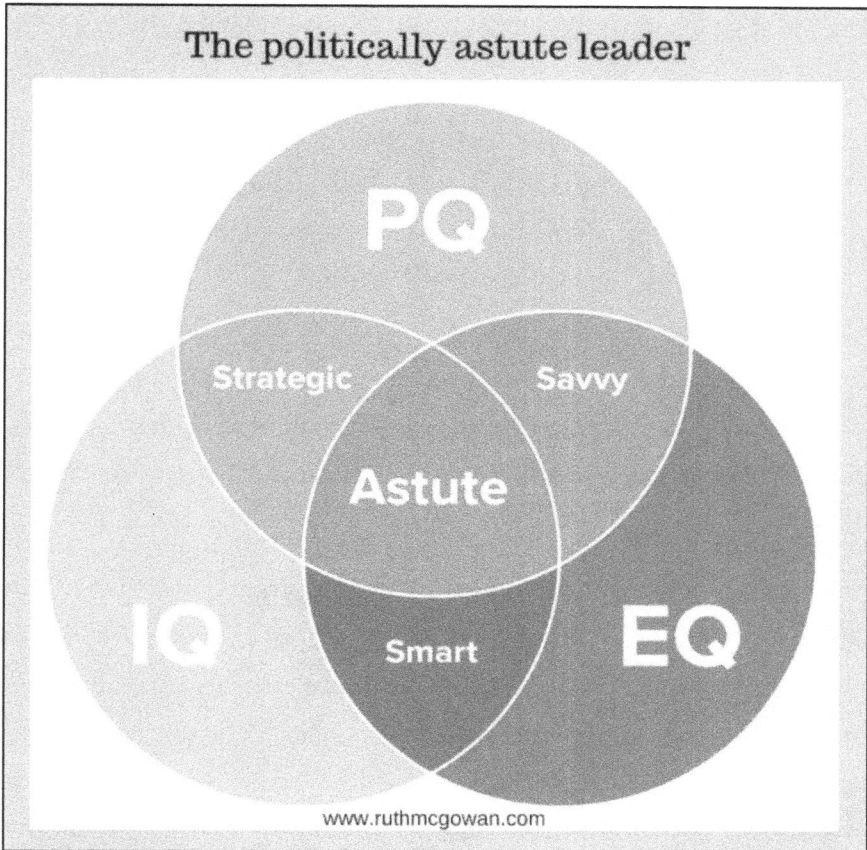

The politically astute leader

PQ

Strategic    Savvy

Astute

IQ

Smart

EQ

www.ruthmcgowan.com

The key is recognizing office politics as a neutral, natural part of professional life, not inherently bad or good. Political skill is about maximizing and leveraging relationships to achieve organizational, team, and individual goals.

Politically savvy leaders can navigate complex organizational dynamics to improve performance, drive productivity, and meet leadership challenges. Political skills enhance a leader's effectiveness, boost team success, and increase one's chances of career advancement.

Sheryl Sandberg, former COO of Facebook (now Meta), is an excellent example of political savvy in business. Sandberg's political acumen was instrumental in helping the company scale from a small startup to a global tech giant.

When Sandberg joined Facebook in 2008, the company was focused on growth but needed a clear business model. She used her political skills to bridge the gap between the tech-focused founders and the financial realities of running a large, publicly traded company. Sandberg built strong relationships with key stakeholders, including CEO Mark Zuckerberg, board members, and senior leaders. She influenced the company's direction by introducing monetization strategies, including developing Facebook's advertising platform, which became one of its most profitable revenue streams.

Her political savvy was also evident in navigating crises, such as the Cambridge Analytica scandal. Sandberg managed internal and external communication effectively and leveraged her network to address the concerns of regulators, investors, and the public. While the situation was challenging, her ability to maintain trust with key stakeholders stabilized the company during a turbulent period.

Sandberg's political skills led Facebook to growth and financial success, cementing her role as one of the most influential figures in Silicon Valley. Understanding how to influence people and organizations, she positioned herself and the company to thrive in an incredibly competitive and dynamic industry.

### Six Characteristics of Politically Skilled Leaders[52]

How can you recognize a politically skilled leader? Ironically, their political abilities often seem invisible. Politically savvy leaders come across as genuine, authentic, and effective rather than manipulative or self-serving.

These leaders skillfully navigate organizational dynamics without drawing attention to their strategies.

Politically adept leaders typically excel in six key characteristics:

*1. Social Astuteness*

Socially astute leaders possess a keen awareness of their surroundings. They have a heightened ability to read and interpret social cues. They excel at picking up nonverbal signals, group dynamics, and underlying motives. This awareness allows them to understand an organization's formal and informal networks. With this skill, they know who holds influence, what motivates different individuals, and how to navigate sensitive political landscapes. Social astuteness helps them adapt their behavior in different settings to maximize their impact, often making decisions or crafting messages that resonate deeply with diverse stakeholders.

*2. Interpersonal Influence*

Leaders with strong interpersonal influence can persuade others without being overbearing or forceful. They tailor their communication style to their audience, fostering rapport and trust. These leaders subtly guide conversations and decision-making to achieve desired outcomes, whether securing buy-in for a project or resolving conflicts. Their influence is built on trust, credibility, and emotional intelligence. They understand that successful leadership involves directing, listening, empathizing, and responding in ways that empower others to follow them willingly.

| | INTERPERSONAL COMMUNICATION | INTRAPERSONAL COMMUNICATION |
|---|---|---|
| Definition | Referring to something that occurs between people | Referring to something that occurs within oneself |
| Who's involved | Two or more people | Just you |
| When does it happen | When you want to communicate with others | When you want to plan, reflect, get closer to yourself |
| Media used | Phone, Computer, TV, In-person, Letters | Mind, Diaries, Audio Recordings |
| Concerned with | Exchange of ideas | Thought and analysis |

*3. Networking Ability*

Networking is essential for politically savvy leaders. They don't just connect with people in their immediate teams; they build relationships across all levels of the organization and with external stakeholders. Their networks encompass individuals from different departments, industries, and backgrounds. This gives them access to a wealth of resources, knowledge, and opportunities they can leverage to advance organizational goals. Politically skilled leaders strategically nurture these connections. They know their network can offer crucial support, information, or collaboration when needed. Strong networking skills enable them to navigate power structures and influence decision-makers beyond their immediate circle.

### 4. Thinking Before Speaking

Politically skilled leaders are thoughtful communicators. They understand the weight of their words and the impact they can have. They carefully consider what to say, how to say it, and when to say it. Rather than reacting impulsively, they pause to reflect, ensuring their message aligns with their goals and the current organizational climate. Their thoughtfulness helps them avoid miscommunication and prevent unnecessary conflicts. Their measured approach to communication enables them to frame ideas in ways that resonate with others, fostering cooperation and reducing resistance.

### 5. Managing Up

Leaders with political savvy are skilled at managing their relationships with those above them. This doesn't mean simply catering to superiors; it requires understanding their boss's priorities, pressures, and working style and positioning oneself as a reliable, strategic partner. Politically skilled leaders know how to keep their superiors informed, manage expectations, and offer solutions aligned with organizational goals. They present ideas in ways that speak to their superiors' concerns. This helps them gain support for their initiatives and build a reputation as someone who can be trusted with more responsibility.

### 6. Apparent Sincerity

The ability to project sincerity is the most critical characteristic of politically savvy leaders. People are likelier to follow and support leaders who genuinely invest in their well-being and the team's success. Apparent sincerity means the leader's actions are perceived as honest and transparent, with no hidden agendas. Even when making politically strategic moves, these leaders come across as authentic, which fosters trust and reduces the likelihood of others feeling manipulated. This sincerity builds long-term credibility, ensuring the leader's influence is sustainable and far-reaching.

Politically skilled leaders combine these six characteristics to navigate the complexities of their organizations effectively. Their ability to leverage social awareness, influence others, build diverse networks, communicate thoughtfully, manage relationships with superiors, and project sincerity makes them highly effective in achieving their personal and organizational goals.

# CONCLUSION

You made it! Congratulations. We've covered a lot. So what do you think?

Did you get some short- and long-term ideas on how to implement them? Some areas you want to research more? A few quotes you'd like to remember? How about some key takeaways? We truly hope so.

Momentum begins **now** as you, the visionary leader, take the strategies within these pages and transform them into action. **The four pillars— wellness, emotional intelligence, communication, and leadership**—are not just theoretical concepts but powerful tools ready to drive your business's success and growth.

To recap, these pillars are the foundation you need for unleashing unprecedented company growth and fostering high-performing, engaged teams…

- **Wellness** ensures that teams are physically and emotionally equipped to do great work.
- **Emotional intelligence** fosters compassion and understanding, which creates trust and reduces conflict.

- **Communication** is the glue that connects people, ensures alignment, and builds collaboration.
- **Leadership** sets the tone, inspires action, and models the behavior every team member strives to emulate.

These pillars are tangible, actionable, and proven strategies. And now that you've finished CULTURE CATALYST, they can be integrated into your business operation to create a culture where your people thrive and profits soar 24/7/365.

Imagine creating an environment where communication flows seamlessly, emotional intelligence guides every interaction and decision, social intelligence builds a cohesive and resilient team, and wellness is prioritized, leading to a motivated and thriving workforce. Each of these pillars supports the other, creating a robust foundation for a culture of positivity and excellence.

Again, we get it! Recall that at the beginning of the book, we asked why creating a great company culture is so difficult for so many organizations.

- We said company culture is notoriously resistant to change. NOW you know that when everyone is on the same page, all working together, all aligned under the same goals, it is EASY.

- We said leaders can face significant pushback when they attempt to introduce new cultural norms or values. NOW you know that when the C-suite or your leadership team and the rest of the organization are aligned, and they feel like the leadership team cares deeply about them, it is EASY.

- We said that leaders may fail to model the desired cultural attributes, creating a disconnect between what leaders say and what they do. NOW you know that for fully evolved leaders who understand the power of a great culture, modeling comes EASY.

- We said that leadership turnover can destabilize company culture. NOW you know that when the leadership team is happy and sharing all the "good stuff" with the rest of the organization, not only do they stay…they stay for a long, long time. And that makes this one EASY, too.

- We said multiple generations and cultural backgrounds coexisting in the same workplace can be a challenge. NOW you know that when there is depth and breadth of emotional wellness and understanding, it is EASY.

- We said that the rise of remote work and globalization have altered the playing field. NOW you know that this change doesn't need to be a deal breaker. Change is inevitable, and this is no longer an issue in a company with a positive culture.

- Finally, we said that attracting and retaining the right talent can be challenging and is intrinsically linked to creating a positive culture. NOW you know that when you are known for your culture, people will beat down a path to your door. As "the" great company to work for, you'll be able to select *the best and the brightest*. And that's a beautiful thing!

So yes, company culture is a **complicated** aspect of business that molds and shapes everything in its path, from human resources to operations, from sales and marketing to organizational performance. *Everything.*

Why? Because culture is about **people**. And relationships can be hard to navigate. But they are *worth it* when you can see that it all becomes very EASY when you prioritize it.

Now with this book in your hand, you have THE TOOLS you need for creating a workplace where everyone on your team **thrives, collaborates, and contributes** to the overall success of the business and…their own workplace joy and satisfaction.

**Your Invitation to Lead360 Academy**

This book also serves as a stepping stone to the comprehensive support that **Lead360 Academy** (Visit *CultureCatalystBook.com* to learn more about our annual course) can provide, ensuring you reach all of your leadership goals and ultimately achieve momentum in your business with growth and success. Remember to always do the following:

1. Challenge yourself and your team to integrate open and honest communication into your daily operations.
2. Cultivate emotional intelligence within your organization to enhance relationships and decision-making.
3. Encourage social intelligence to foster collaboration and understanding among your team members.
4. Prioritize wellness to boost productivity and engagement across the board.

Transformation begins with **action**. By implementing these pillars, you are elevating your business to new heights and setting a precedent for a sustainable, fulfilling work environment. Lead with intention, inspire with vision, and watch your team and business thrive beyond measure! Your leadership journey is an ongoing adventure. Embrace it with courage and passion, and continue evolving, adapting, and learning. The path to **greatness** is paved by those who dare to lead authentically and purposefully.

As you move forward, know you have the tools and the power to make a profound impact. Here's to your success and the incredible journey ahead!

*-Tiffany & Marni*

# INTEGRATION INDEX

Short-term ideas to implement (30 days or less)

# INTEGRATION INDEX

Long-term ideas to implement (90 days or less)

# INTEGRATION INDEX

Things I want to research more

# INTEGRATION INDEX

Quotes I'd like to remember

# INTEGRATION INDEX

Takeaways

# END NOTES

[1] https://www.forbes.com/sites/benjaminlaker/2021/04/23/culture-is-a-companys-single-most-powerful-advantage-heres-why/

[2] https://groups.chicagobooth.edu/boothwellness/what-is-wellness/

[3] https://www.shrm.org/topics-tools/news/hr-magazine/1006-hr-magazine-eaps-diverse-world

[4] https://pubmed.ncbi.nlm.nih.gov/2000322/

[5] https://pubmed.ncbi.nlm.nih.gov/9748973/

[6] https://www.kff.org/private-insurance/issue-brief/trends-in-workplace-wellness-programs-and-evolving-federal-standards/

[7] https://pubmed.ncbi.nlm.nih.gov/16018536/

[8] https://journals.sagepub.com/doi/abs/10.1177/1524839909349162

[9] https://www.simplypsychology.org/maslow.html

[10] https://www.bls.gov/tus/home.htm

[11] https://pmc.ncbi.nlm.nih.gov/articles/PMC5081153/

[12] https://www.cdc.gov/workplace-health-promotion/media/pdfs/2024/08/physicalactivity-employerguide-508.pdf

[13] https://news.gallup.com/poll/357749/mental-health-rating-remains-below-pre-pandemic-level.aspx

[14] https://www.psychologytoday.com/us/blog/frazzlebrain/202305/how-to-overcome-self-doubt-and-flourish

[15] https://www.nih.gov/health-information/emotional-wellness-toolkit

[16] https://newsinhealth.nih.gov/2022/04/nurture-your-resilience

[17] https://www.nih.gov/sites/default/files/health-info/wellness-toolkits/emotional-wellness-checklist-2022-7.pdf

[18] https://newsinhealth.nih.gov/2021/01/feeling-stressed

[19] https://newsinhealth.nih.gov/2021/01/feeling-stressed

[20] https://pubmed.ncbi.nlm.nih.gov/30827911/

[21] https://www.nih.gov/news-events/nih-research-matters/how-sleep-clears-brain

[22] https://newsinhealth.nih.gov/2021/04/good-sleep-good-health

[23] https://newsinhealth.nih.gov/2021/06/mindfulness-your-health

[24] https://www.unh.edu/health/spiritual-wellness

[25] https://www.unh.edu/health/occupational-wellness

[26] https://www.unh.edu/health/intellectual-wellness

[27] https://www.gallup.com/workplace/349484/state-of-the-global-workplace.aspx

[28] https://www.unh.edu/health/environmental-wellness

[29] https://ewcstatic.thehartford.com/thehartford/the_hartford/files/GB/future-of-benefits-executive-summary-2023.pdf

[30] https://www.myshortlister.com/insights/employee-financial-stress-in-the-workplace

[31] https://www.unh.edu/health/financial-wellness

[32] https://online.hbs.edu/blog/post/emotional-intelligence-in-leadership

[33] https://hbr.org/2018/01/what-self-awareness-really-is-and-how-to-cultivate-it

[34] https://www.linkedin.com/pulse/what-impact-unresolved-workplace-conflicts-employee-denicola-/

[35] https://pmc.ncbi.nlm.nih.gov/articles/PMC8848120/

[36] https://pmc.ncbi.nlm.nih.gov/articles/PMC4116082/

[37] https://dialecticalbehaviortherapy.com/

[38] https://marcbrackett.com/ruler/

[39] https://www.gallup.com/workplace/643286/engagement-hits-11-year-low.aspx

[40] https://www.linkedin.com/posts/paul-derby-2502917_journalism-corporatecommunications-storytelling-activity-7269290972142874625-sofd/

[41] https://hbr.org/1991/05/teaching-smart-people-how-to-learn

[42] https://health.clevelandclinic.org/passive-aggressive

[43] https://www.simplypsychology.org/passive-aggressive-behavior.html

[44] https://www.berkeleywellbeing.com/passive-aggression.html

[45] https://roubler.com/resources/blog/written-communication/

[46] https://ifvp.org/content/why-our-brain-loves-pictures

[47] Jensen, Susan & Luthans, Fred. (2006). Entrepreneurs as Authentic Leaders: Impact on Employees' Attitudes. Leadership & Organization Development Journal. 27. 10.1108/01437730610709273.

[48] https://online.hbs.edu/blog/post/authentic-leadership

[49] https://www.cdfifund.gov/sites/cdfi/files/documents/(51)-leadership-that-gets-results.pdf

[50] https://www.cdfifund.gov/sites/cdfi/files/documents/(51)-leadership-that-gets-results.pdf

[51] https://www.ccl.org/articles/leading-effectively-articles/4-keys-strengthen-ability-influence-others/#:~:text=By%20definition%2C%20influence%20is%20the,skills%20needed%20in%20every%20role

[52] https://www.ccl.org/articles/leading-effectively-articles/6-aspects-of-political-skill/